Multiple Intelligences

GRADE **K**

teaching kids the way they learn

written by
Irene A. Paredes Barnett

Cover by Dawn Devries Sokol
Interior illustrations by Kay McCabe and Kelly McMahon
Symbol design by Rose Sheifer

FS-23279 Multiple Intelligences: Teaching Kids the Way They Learn Kindergarten
All rights reserved. Printed in the U.S.A.
Copyright © 1999 Frank Schaffer Publications, Inc.
23740 Hawthorne Blvd., Torrance, CA 90505

TABLE of CONTENTS

What Is the Multiple Intelligences Theory?

The Multiple Intelligences Theory, developed and researched by Dr. Howard Gardner, recognizes the multifaceted profile of the human mind. In his book *Frames of Mind* (Basic Books, 1993) Dr. Gardner explains that every human possesses several intelligences in greater or lesser degrees. Each person is born with a unique intelligence profile and uses any or all of these intelligences to acquire knowledge and experience.

At present Gardner has defined eight intelligences. Below are the intelligences and a simplified definition of each. A more complete explanation of each intelligence is found at the end of the introduction.

- verbal-linguistic: word intelligence
- logical-mathematical: number and reasoning intelligence
- visual-spatial: picture intelligence
- musical-rhythmic: music and rhythm intelligence
- bodily-kinesthetic: body intelligence
- interpersonal: social intelligence
- intrapersonal: self intelligence
- naturalist: natural environment intelligence

Gardner stresses that although intelligence is a biological function, it is inseparable from the cultural context in which it exists. He cites the example of Bobby Fischer, the chess champion. In a culture without chess, Fischer would not have been able to become a good chess player.

The Multiple Intelligences Theory in the Classroom

The Multiple Intelligences Theory has been making its way into the educational setting over the past decade. Instinctively, educators have recognized that their students learn differently, respond uniquely to a variety of teaching techniques, and have their individual preferences. Traditional educational programs do not recognize the unique intelligence profile of each student. Traditionally educators have operated according to the belief that there is a single type of intelligence, based on a combination of math and verbal ability. This more one-dimensional view gave rise to the commonly held definition of an "IQ." According to this definition, all individuals are born with this general ability and it does not change with age, training, or experience. Dr. Gardner's theory plays a significant role in rethinking how to educate so as to meet each student's individual needs. Basic skills can be more effectively acquired if all of a student's strengths are involved in the learning process.

The key to lesson design for a multiple intelligences learning environment is to reflect on the concept you want to teach and identify the intelligences that seem most appropriate for communicating the content. At Mountlake Terrace High School in Edmonds, Washington, Eeva Reeder's math students learn about algebraic equations kinesthetically by using the pavement in the school's yard like a giant graph. Using the large, square cement blocks of the pavement, they identify the axes, the X and Y coordinates, and plot themselves as points on the axes.

Other teachers will attempt to engage all eight intelligences in their lessons by using learning centers to focus on different approaches to the same concept. An example of this is Bruce Campbell's third grade classroom in Marysville, Washington. Campbell, a consultant on teaching through multiple intelligences, has designed a unit on Planet Earth that includes seven centers: a building center where students use clay to make models of the earth; a math center; a reading center; a music center where students study unit spelling words while listening to music; an art center using concentric circle patterns; a cooperative learning activity; a writing center titled "Things I would take with me on a journey to the center of the earth."

Another way to use the multiple intelligences theory in the classroom is through student projects. For example, Barbara Hoffman had her third-grade students in Country Day School in Costa Rica develop games in small groups. The students had to determine the objective and rules of the game. They researched questions and answers and designed and assembled a game board and accessories. Many intelligences were engaged through the creation of this project.

Dr. Gardner recommends that schools personalize their programs by providing apprenticeships. These should be designed to allow students to pursue their interests, with an emphasis on acquiring expertise over a period of time. In the Escuela Internacional Valle del Sol in Costa Rica, apprenticeships based on the eight intelligences are used. In one program long-term special subjects are offered to students in areas such as cooking, soccer, and drama. In addition, at the end of the term the entire school participates in a special project in multiage grouping with activities focused around a theme such as Egypt or European medieval life.

Assessment

The multiple intelligences theory challenges us to redefine assessment and see it as an integral part of the learning process. Dr. Gardner believes that many of the intelligences do not lend themselves to being measured by standardized paper and pencil tests. In a classroom structured on the multiple intelligences theory, assessment is integrated with learning and instruction and stimulates further learning. The teacher, the student, and his or her peers are involved in ongoing assessment. In this way the student has a better understanding of his or her strengths and weaknesses. Self-evaluation gives students the opportunity to set goals, to use higher-order thinking skills, as well as to generalize and personalize what they learn.

One example of nontraditional assessment is the development and maintenance of student portfolios, including drafts, sketches, and final products. Both student and teacher choose pieces that illustrate the student's growth. (Gardner calls these *process folios*.) Self-assessment can also include parental assessment, as well as watching videotaped student performances, and students editing or reviewing each other's work.

How to Use This Book

Multiple Intelligences: Teaching Kids the Way They Learn Kindergarten is designed to assist teachers in implementing this theory across the curriculum. This book is for teachers of students in kindergarten. It is divided into six subject areas: language arts, social studies, mathematics, science, fine arts, and physical education. Each subject area offers a collection of practical, creative ideas for teaching each of the eight intelligences. The book also offers reproducible student worksheets to supplement many of these activities. (A small image of the worksheet can be found next to the activity it supplements.) Teachers may pick and choose from the various activities to develop a multiple intelligences program that meets their students' needs.

The activities are designed to help the teacher engage all the intelligences during the learning process so that the unique qualities of each student are recognized, encouraged, and cultivated. The activities provide opportunities for students to explore their individual interests and talents while learning the basic knowledge and skills that all must master. Each activity focuses on one intelligence; however, other intelligences will come into play since the intelligences naturally interact with each other.

As a teacher, you have the opportunity to provide a variety of educational experiences that can help students excel in their studies as well as discover new and exciting abilities and strengths within themselves. Your role in the learning process can provide students with an invaluable opportunity to fulfill their potential and enrich their lives.

Words of Advice

The following are some tips to assist you in using the Multiple Intelligences Theory in your classroom.

- Examine your own strengths and weaknesses in each of the intelligences. Call on others to help you expand your lessons to address the entire range of intelligences.

- Spend time in the early weeks of the school year working with your students to evaluate their comfort and proficiency within the various intelligences. Use your knowledge of their strengths to design and implement your teaching strategies.

- Refrain from "pigeonholing" your students into limited areas of intelligence. Realize that a student can grow from an activity that is not stressing his or her dominant intelligence.

- Work on goal-setting with students and help them develop plans to attain their goals.

- Develop a variety of assessment strategies and record-keeping tools.

- Flexibility is essential. The Multiple Intelligences Theory can be applied in a myriad of ways. There is no one right way.

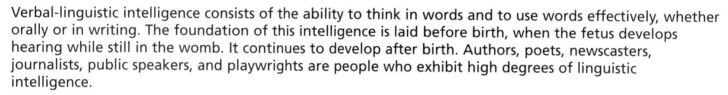

The Eight Intelligences

Below is a brief definition of each of the eight intelligences, along with tips on how to recognize the characteristics of each and how to develop these intelligences in your students.

Verbal-Linguistic Intelligence

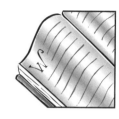

Verbal-linguistic intelligence consists of:

- a sensitivity to semantics—the meaning of words
- a sensitivity to syntax—the order among words
- a sensitivity to phonology—the sounds, rhythms, and inflections of words
- a sensitivity to the different functions of language, including its potential to excite, convince, stimulate, convey information, or please

Verbal-linguistic intelligence consists of the ability to think in words and to use words effectively, whether orally or in writing. The foundation of this intelligence is laid before birth, when the fetus develops hearing while still in the womb. It continues to develop after birth. Authors, poets, newscasters, journalists, public speakers, and playwrights are people who exhibit high degrees of linguistic intelligence.

People who are strongly linguistic like to read, write, tell stories or jokes, and play word games. They enjoy listening to stories or to people talking. They may have a good vocabulary or a good memory for names, places, dates, and trivia. They may spell words accurately and communicate to others effectively. They might also exhibit the ability to learn other languages.

Verbal-linguistic intelligence can be stimulated and developed in the classroom by providing a language rich environment. Classrooms in every subject area should include activities to help students develop a passion for language through speaking, hearing, reading, and examining words. Have students write stories, poems, jokes, letters, or journals. Provide opportunities for impromptu speaking, rapping, debate, storytelling, oral reading, silent reading, choral reading, and oral presentations. Involve students in class discussions and encourage them to ask questions and listen. Invite students to use storyboards, tape recorders, and word processors. Plan field trips to libraries, newspapers, or bookstores. Supply nontraditional materials such as comics and crossword puzzles to interest reluctant students.

Writing, listening, reading, and speaking effectively are key skills. The development of these four parts of linguistic intelligence can have a significant effect on a student's success in learning all subject areas and throughout life.

Logical-Mathematical Intelligence

Logical-mathematical intelligence consists of:

- the ability to use numbers effectively
- the ability to use inductive and deductive reasoning
- the ability to recognize abstract patterns

This intelligence encompasses three broad, interrelated fields: math, science, and logic. It begins when young children confront the physical objects of the world and ends with the understanding of abstract ideas. Throughout this process, a person develops a capacity to discern logical or numerical patterns and to handle long chains of reasoning. Scientists, mathematicians, computer programmers, bankers, accountants, and lawyers exhibit high degrees of logical-mathematical intelligence.

People with well-developed logical-mathematical intelligence like to find patterns and relationships among objects or numbers. They enjoy playing strategy games such as chess or checkers, solving riddles, and logical puzzles or brain teasers. They organize or categorize things and ask questions about how things work. These people easily solve math problems quickly in their heads. They may have a good sense of cause and effect and think on a more abstract or conceptual level.

Logical-mathematical intelligence can be stimulated and developed in the classroom by providing an environment in which students frequently experiment, classify, categorize, and analyze. Have students notice and work with numbers across the curriculum. Provide activities that focus on outlining, analogies, deciphering codes, or finding patterns and relationships.

Most adults use logical-mathematical intelligence in their daily lives to calculate household budgets, to make decisions, and to solve problems. Most professions depend in some way on this intelligence because it encompasses many kinds of thinking. The development of logical-mathematical intelligence benefits all aspects of life.

Bodily-Kinesthetic Intelligence

Bodily-kinesthetic intelligence consists of:

- the ability to control one's body movements to express ideas and feelings
- the capacity to handle objects skillfully, including the use of both fine and gross motor movements
- the ability to learn by movement, interaction, and participation

Bodily-kinesthetic intelligence begins with the control of automatic and voluntary movement and progresses to using the body in highly differentiated ways. The skillful manipulation of one's body or an object requires an acute sense of timing and direction, as well as the ability to transform an intention into action. Examples of people who possess bodily-kinesthetic intelligence are a dancer using his or her body as an object for expressive purposes and a basketball player who manipulates a ball with finesse. This intelligence can be seen in inventors, mechanics, actors, surgeons, swimmers, and artists.

People who are strongly bodily-kinesthetic enjoy working with their hands, have good coordination, and handle tools skillfully. They enjoy taking things apart and putting them back together. They prefer to manipulate objects to solve problems. They move, twitch, tap, or fidget while seated for a long time. They cleverly mimic other's gestures.

Many people find it difficult to understand and retain information that is taught only through their visual and auditory modes. They must manipulate or experience what they learn in order to understand and remember information. Bodily-kinesthetic individuals learn through doing and through multi-sensory experiences.

Bodily-kinesthetic intelligence can be stimulated and developed in the classroom through activities that involve physical movements such as role-playing, drama, mime, charades, dance, sports, and exercise. Have your students put on plays, puppet shows, or dance performances. Provide opportunities for students to manipulate and touch objects through activities such as painting, clay modeling, or building. Plan field trips to the theater, art museum, ballet, craft shows, and parks.

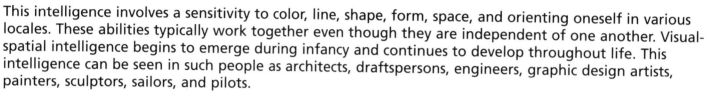

Visual-Spatial Intelligence

Visual-spatial intelligence consists of:

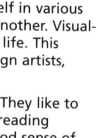

- the ability to perceive the visual-spatial world accurately
- the ability to think in pictures or visual imagery
- the ability to graphically represent visual or spatial ideas
- the ability to orient the body in space

This intelligence involves a sensitivity to color, line, shape, form, space, and orienting oneself in various locales. These abilities typically work together even though they are independent of one another. Visual-spatial intelligence begins to emerge during infancy and continues to develop throughout life. This intelligence can be seen in such people as architects, draftspersons, engineers, graphic design artists, painters, sculptors, sailors, and pilots.

Spatially skilled people enjoy art activities, jigsaw or visual perception puzzles, and mazes. They like to construct three-dimensional models. These people get more out of pictures than words in reading materials. They may excel at reading maps, charts, and diagrams. Also, they may have a good sense of direction.

Visual-spatial intelligence can be stimulated and developed in the classroom by providing a visually rich environment in which students frequently focus on images, pictures, and color. Provide opportunities for reading maps and charts, drawing diagrams and illustrations, constructing models, painting, coloring, and solving puzzles. Play games that require visual memory or spatial acuity. Use guided imagery, pretending, or active imagination exercises to have students solve problems. Use videos, slides, posters, charts, diagrams, telescopes, or color-coded material to teach the content area. Visit art museums, historical buildings, or planetariums.

Visual-spatial intelligence is an object-based intelligence. It functions in the concrete world, the world of objects and their locations. This intelligence underlies all human activity.

Musical Intelligence

Musical intelligence consists of:

- a sensitivity to pitch (melody), rhythm, and timbre (tone)
- an appreciation of musical expressiveness
- an ability to express oneself through music, rhythm, or dance

Dr. Gardner asserts that of all forms of intelligence, the consciousness-altering effect of musical intelligence is probably the greatest because of the impact of music on the state of the brain. He suggests that any normal individual who has had frequent exposure to music can manipulate pitch, rhythm, and timbre to participate with some skill in composing, singing, or playing instruments. The early childhood years appear to be the most crucial period for musical growth. This intelligence can be seen in composers, conductors, instrumentalists, singers, and dancers.

Musically skilled people may remember the melodies of songs. They may have a good singing voice and tap rhythmically on a surface. Also, they may unconsciously hum to themselves and may be able to identify when musical notes are off-key. They enjoy singing songs, listening to music, playing an instrument, or attending musical performances.

Musical intelligence can be stimulated and developed in the classroom by providing opportunities to listen to musical recordings, to create and play musical instruments, or to sing and dance. Let students express their feelings or thoughts through using musical instruments, songs, or jingles. Play background music while the students are working. Plan field trips to the symphony, a recording studio, a musical, or an opera.

There are strong connections between music and emotions. By having music in the classroom, a positive emotional environment conducive to learning can be created. Lay the foundations of musical intelligence in your classroom by using music throughout the school day.

Interpersonal Intelligence

Interpersonal intelligence consists of:

- the ability to focus outward to other individuals
- the ability to sense other people's moods, temperaments, motivations, and intentions
- the ability to communicate, cooperate, and collaborate with others

In the early form of this intelligence, a young child possesses the ability to discriminate among the individuals around him or her and to detect their various moods. In the more advanced form of this intelligence, one can read the intentions and desires of other individuals and act upon that knowledge. This intelligence includes the ability to form and maintain relationships and to assume various roles within groups. The competence is prominent in political and religious leaders, salespeople, teachers, counselors, social workers, and therapists.

Interpersonally skilled people have the capacity to influence their peers and often excel at group work, team efforts, and collaborative projects. They enjoy social interaction and are sensitive to the feelings and moods of others. They tend to take leadership roles in activities with friends and often belong to clubs and other organizations.

Interpersonal intelligence can be developed and strengthened through maintaining a warm, accepting, supporting classroom environment. Provide opportunities for students to collaboratively work in groups. Have students peer teach and contribute to group discussions. Involve the students in situations where they have to be active listeners, be aware of other's feelings, motives, and opinions, and show empathy.

The positive development of interpersonal intelligence is an important step toward leading a successful and fulfilling life. Interpersonal intelligence is called upon in our daily lives as we interact with others in our communities, environments, nations, and world.

Intrapersonal Intelligence

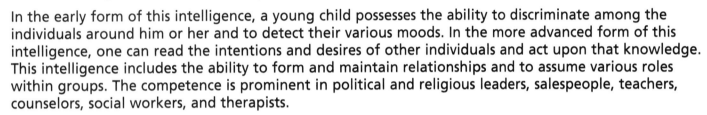

Intrapersonal intelligence consists of:

- the ability to look inward to examine one's own thoughts and feelings
- the ability to control one's thoughts and emotions and consciously work with them
- the ability to express one's inner life
- the drive toward self-actualization

This intelligence focuses on the ability to develop a complete model of oneself, including one's desires, goals, anxieties, strengths, and limitations, and also to draw upon that model as a means of understanding and guiding one's behavior. In its basic form, it is the ability to distinguish a feeling of pleasure from one of pain, and to make a determination to either continue or withdraw from a situation based on this feeling. In the more advanced form of this intelligence, one has the ability to detect and to symbolize complex and highly differentiated sets of feelings. Some individuals with strong intrapersonal intelligence are philosophers, spiritual counselors, psychiatrists, and wise elders.

Intrapersonally skilled people are aware of their range of emotions and have a realistic sense of their strengths and weaknesses. They prefer to work independently and often have their own style of living and learning. They are able to accurately express their feelings and have a good sense of self-direction. They possess high self-confidence.

Intrapersonal intelligence can be developed through maintaining a warm, caring, nurturing environment that promotes self-esteem. Offer activities that require independent learning and imagination. During the school day, provide students with quiet time and private places to work and reflect. Provide long-term, meaningful learning projects that allow students to explore their interests and abilities. Encourage students to maintain portfolios, examine and make sense of their work. Involve students in activities that require them to explore their values, beliefs, and feelings.

Intrapersonal intelligence requires a lifetime of living and learning to inwardly know, be, and accept oneself. The classroom is a place where teachers can help students begin this journey of self-knowledge. Developing intrapersonal intelligence has far-reaching effects, since self-knowledge underlies success and fulfillment in life.

Naturalist Intelligence

Naturalist intelligence consists of:

- the ability to understand, appreciate, and enjoy the natural world
- the ability to observe, understand, and organize patterns in the natural environment
- the ability to nurture plants and animals

This intelligence focuses on the ability to recognize and classify the many different organic and inorganic species. Paleontologists, forest rangers, horticulturists, zoologists, and meteorologists exhibit naturalist intelligence.

People who exhibit strength in the naturalist intelligence are very much at home in nature. They enjoy being outdoors, camping, and hiking, as well as studying and learning about animals and plants. They can easily classify and identify various species.

Naturalist intelligence can be developed and strengthened through activities that involve hands-on labs, creating classroom habitats, caring for plants and animals, and classifying and discriminating species. Encourage your students to collect and classify seashells, insects, rocks, or other natural phenomena. Visit a museum of natural history, a university life sciences department, or nature center.

Naturalist intelligence enhances our lives. The more we know about the natural world, and the more we are able to recognize patterns in our environment, the better perspective we have on our role in natural cycles and our place in the universe.

REFERENCES

Armstrong, Thomas. *Multiple Intelligences in the Classroom*. Alexandria, VA: Assoc. for Supervision and Curriculum Development, 1994. A good overview of the Multiple Intelligences Theory and how to explore, introduce, and develop lessons on this theory.

Campbell, Linda, Bruce Campbell, and Dee Dickerson. *Teaching and Learning Through Multiple Intelligences*. Needham Heights, MA: Allyn and Bacon, 1996. An overview and resource of teaching strategies in musical, spatial, bodily-kinesthetic, interpersonal, and intrapersonal intelligences.

Gardner, Howard. *Frames of Mind: The Theory of Multiple Intelligences*. New York: Basic Books, 1993. A detailed analysis and explanation of the Multiple Intelligences Theory.

———. *Multiple Intelligences: The Theory in Practice*. New York: Basic Books, 1993. This book provides a coherent picture of what Gardner and his colleagues have learned about the educational applications of the Multiple Intelligences Theory over the last decade. It provides an overview of the theory and examines its implications for assessment and teaching from preschool to college admissions.

Haggerty, Brian A. *Nurturing Intelligences: A Guide to Multiple Intelligences Theory and Teaching*. Menlo Park, CA: Innovative Learning, Addison-Wesley, 1995. Principles, practical suggestions, and examples for applying the Multiple Intelligences Theory in the classroom. Exercises, problems, and puzzles introduce each of the seven intelligences.

Lazear, David. *Seven Pathways of Learning: Teaching Students and Parents About Multiple Intelligences*. Tucson: Zephyr Press, 1994. Assists in strengthening the child's personal intelligence and in integrating multiple intelligences into everyday life. Includes reproducibles and activities to involve parents.

———. *Seven Ways of Knowing: Teaching for Multiple Intelligences*. Arlington Heights, IL: IRI/SkyLight Training and Pub., 1992. A survey of the theory of multiple intelligences with many general activities for awakening and developing the intelligences.

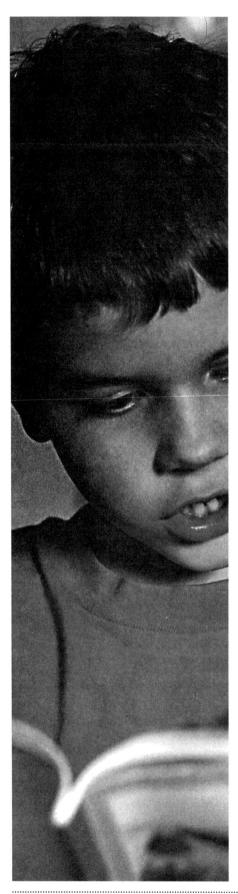

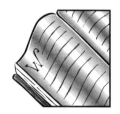

Verbal-Linguistic Intelligence

Kindergarten Post Office

In this activity, students will experience the fun of sending and receiving correspondence as they create a classroom post office. Have each student bring an old shoe box to school. Carefully use a matte cutter or pair of scissors to cut a pull-down flap on the end of each student's box. Make sure the opening is large enough for an envelope to pass through. Have each student print his or her name on the pull-down flap of the box. Then glue or tape the boxes together to form the mailboxes of the classroom post office.

Bring a few sample pieces of mail to the classroom for students to study, such as a postcard, a letter from a friend, a sale brochure, and a magazine. Introduce your students to all the different kinds of mail. Explain that some mail contains important information and may require the person to write a letter in response. Show students the sample postcard. Point out that postcards usually have a photograph or drawing on one side. On the other side there is space for writing a note, a place for the name and address of the person the post card will go to, and a place for a stamp.

Give each student a copy of the **Kindergarten Postcard** worksheet on page 19. Tell students that they can mail postcards to each other. Have students cut out the postcards. Provide crayons, colored markers, or pencils, and have students draw a picture on the blank side of the postcard. The drawing can be of themselves, their friends, or any other picture they would like to share with a friend.

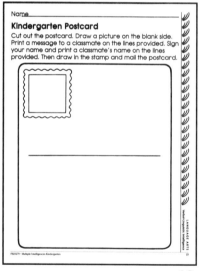

page 19

Then have them write a classmate's name on the back. To ensure that all students receive mail, have them pull names out of a bag. This will also help them in spelling their classmates' names. Tell students they can print a short message on the left side of the postcard. Write a model message on the chalkboard for students to copy. Then let students deliver their postcards to their classmate's mailbox at the classroom post office.

Story Time

Turn off the lights. Light a candle. (If your school doesn't allow candles, use a battery-powered plastic candle—the kind used in windows during the winter

holidays.) Drape a shawl around your shoulders and invite the children to listen to you tell a story. Choose a story that you know very well, and be sure to use character voices and lots of expression.

When finished telling the story, accept your applause. Extinguish the candle and turn on the lights. Invite each child to tell you one thing that he or she enjoyed about your performance and one way that it could be improved. Have the children use "I" statements in their response to you, such as, "I enjoyed the way you used that scary voice when you were the wolf." Or, "I think it would be more interesting if you looked at us more when you talked."

Come for Tea

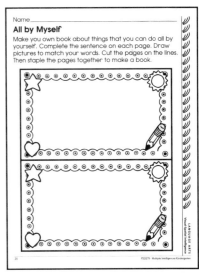

After children have become very familiar with a story, such as "Goldilocks and the Three Bears," invite two children to have a tea party in front of the class, with each child posing as a character in the story. What would they talk about? Imagine Baby Bear talking to Goldilocks! Be sure to have real cups and saucers as props, and allow children to dress up to help them in their role-playing. This activity is sure to help promote comprehension, as children must be true to their characters and the story. For example, if Baby Bear wants to know why Goldilocks broke his chair, she can't deny it, or say it was broken when she got there!

All by Themselves

Read Mercer Mayer's *All By Myself* (Western, 1985). Have the children brainstorm all the things they can do by themselves now that they're in kindergarten. Write these things on the board. Make several copies for each child of the **All by Myself** worksheet on page 20 so that children can make their own mini-books of things they can do by themselves. Have them copy from the list on the board. Then encourage them to read their books to each other. Next discuss and write down the things that the children want to learn to do by the end of kindergarten. They can add pages to the book as they accomplish these things.

Class Journal

Obtain a stuffed animal for the class, such as a teddy bear, or any other toy creature, and name it. Put the stuffed animal in a small box that will also hold a journal. Each child will have a turn at taking the box and contents home for the weekend. The child is to have a parent help him write in the journal about the animal's activities.

page 20

You could start off the journal to give the students an example of what could be written: *Theodore the bear and I went for a wagon ride. We fed some ducks at the pond. We both took a nap and then visited a neighbor. Theodore began collecting leaves. . . .*

My Address

Help your students begin to learn their addresses by having them first draw a picture of their home. Give the children index cards with their addresses on them and ask them to copy their address on the paper they drew on. Place these drawings on a bulletin board entitled *Our Neighborhood.*

Logical-Mathematical Intelligence

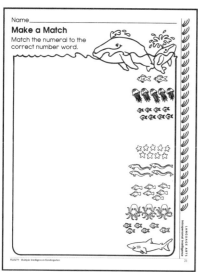

page 21

Alphabet Card Games

Use 52 index cards to make an alphabet deck. Write one uppercase letter on each of 26 cards. Write one lowercase letter on the remaining cards. Your students can practice matching the upper- and lowercase letters by placing them facedown and playing "Concentration." This can be done with pairs or teams, also. To make the game easier, the letters can be put on colored cards. The colors will help children remember the location of the cards.

Teach number words–*one, two, three,* etc.– by creating cards of the number words and corresponding numerals for students to match. To reinforce numeral words, have students do the **Make a Match** worksheet on page 21.

Poetry Patterns

Show students examples of rhyming patterns with simple nursery rhyme verses. Then have them continue the rhyming patterns by coming up with new words that rhyme. Write their words on the board.

Start the activity by showing the class a simple AB pattern such as the following:

One, Two, Three, Four, Five

One, two, three, four, five,

Once I caught a fish alive.

Six, seven, eight, nine, ten,

Then I let it go again.

Why did you let it go?

Because it bit my finger so.

Which finger did it bite?

The little finger on the right.

Mother Goose, illustrated by Gyo Fujikawa (Grosset and Dunlop, 1982), is a good source of rhymes. Rhyming poetry can also be found in *Jaha and*

Jamil Went Down the Hill: An African Mother Goose, by Virginia Kroll (Charlesbridge, 1995), and *Something BIG Has Been Here,* by Jack Prelutsky (Greenwillow, 1990).

 Bodily-Kinesthetic Intelligence

Disappearing Ink

First ask the children to write simple spelling words on one-by-two-inch strips of tag board. Put them in clean yogurt containers with lids.

Invite children to bring their yogurt cup, a plastic cup, and a clean paintbrush outside on the sunny sidewalk or blacktop. Fill each plastic cup with water. Have each child take a word out of his or her yogurt container. Then have him or her "paint" the word on the ground with water and the brush. The children should paint each word in capital and small letters. Be sure to have them check the spelling before the word disappears!

Follow the Capital Letter

For a child, learning the shape of each letter of the alphabet is a little like learning the pathway through a maze. In this activity, students will walk the outline of various alphabet letters to help visualize them.

Cut lengths of wide, brightly colored tape and use them to form a few large letters on the floor of the classroom. Make each letter large enough so that students will be able to walk along the tape that forms each letter.

Tape a green construction-paper circle at the point where students should start to walk each letter. Write the word *go* on the green circle. (For durability, you may want to laminate or cover the construction-paper circles with clear contact paper.) Draw an arrow on each green circle to show the direction the students should walk to complete the letter form. Tape yellow construction-paper triangles at places where students should turn or where the letter has a curve. Draw arrows on the triangles to indicate the direction the students should turn. Then tape a red construction-paper square with the word *stop* written on it where the letter form ends.

Encourage students to orally describe their walks on the letter forms. Ask them to tell if they are walking a straight line, turning to make a curve, or stopping at the red square.

After they have had an opportunity to walk on a few letter forms, ask students to work with a partner. Tell the partners to take turns closing their eyes and letting their partner guide them through the letter form. Ask the students to feel the form he or she is walking. After the student completes the walk, have the student guess the letter he or she has walked.

Visual-Spatial Intelligence

Picture Me a Story

In this activity, students will be asked to retell a familiar story with pictures using the story's setting, characters, and sequence of events.

Read a familiar classic tale to your students, such as "The Three Little Pigs," "Goldilocks and the Three Bears," or "Hansel and Gretel." Tell students to listen to the story carefully as you read it because they will be retelling the story later and drawing pictures of it.

Provide students with paper, crayons, or colored markers. After you have finished telling the story, ask students to think about where the story takes place. Encourage them to describe the story's setting. Have them use the crayons or markers to draw the story's setting.

Next, ask students to name the characters in the story. Have student volunteers describe the different characters. Tell students to draw the characters.

Then ask students to tell what happened in the story. Encourage students to use their own words to tell about the sequence of events in the story. Let students refer to their drawings to tell what happened first, next, and last.

A Dictionary of My Own

In this activity, students will learn how dictionaries are used. They will also make a dictionary of their own.

Show students a picture dictionary and a text-only dictionary. Discuss alphabetizing. Explain that dictionaries are used to learn information about words. Point to a picture in the picture dictionary and have a student volunteer read the picture label. Explain that children can use a picture dictionary by looking at a picture and by reading the words next to the picture.

Show students a page from a text-only dictionary. Explain that most of the time, people look at dictionaries to learn about what words mean–definitions. Tell students that people also look in dictionaries to learn about a word's spelling, its word parts (syllables), and its pronunciation. Tell students that a dictionary is an important tool for writers and readers to use, and that they will be using dictionaries more and more as they get older.

Provide fourteen sheets of blank paper for each child. Staple the sheets together along the left side to make a book. Provide crayons, colored markers, and pencils for students to use to illustrate the covers of their dictionaries. Show them how to write *My Dictionary* on the cover. Then, with the alphabet in sight on the blackboard or bulletin board, ask students to make an uppercase and lowercase letter on the top left corner of each page, following the order of the alphabet.

Provide old magazines, scissors, and glue so students can cut out pictures to glue into their dictionaries. Tell students to find at least one picture for each letter of the alphabet. To make the process go faster, assign letters to each child. When a student finds a picture, it can be photocopied for the entire class. Remind students to label each picture and place it in their dictionary according to the first letter of the word. Encourage them to make drawings when a picture cannot be found.

Musical Intelligence

Over on the Playground

Creating new lyrics to familiar songs is a fun and creative way for children to use language. In this activity, students will help create a song and sing along in a group to the tune of "Over in the Meadow." First introduce the traditional counting verse.

Over in the Meadow

Over in the meadow in the sand in the sun,

Lived Old Mother Turtle and her little turtle one.

"Wink," said his mother. "I wink," said the one.

So they winked and they blinked in the sand in the sun.

Write the modified verse below on the board, leaving blanks in place of the bold words.

Over on the playground in the sand in the sun,

Stood a teacher, (Your Name), and a little student one.

"Jump," said the teacher. "I jump," said the one,

So they jumped and they blinked in the sand in the sun.

Ask students to brainstorm a list of action words. Write the words on the board at the side of the verse. Students will then sing the song. Allow one student to stand and say the action word at the appropriate time during the song. Sing the song until each student has had a chance to stand and say the word, reusing the action words if necessary.

Interpersonal Intelligence

Alphabet Cooperative

Assign each student a large letter of the alphabet that can be hand-held or worn on a construction paper hat. Ask students to line up in the order of the alphabet. (Some students may have to be assigned more than one letter.) Begin the activity by calling out the letter A, B, C and so on, and having the students line up as you call their letter. Have the children take their seats and then form the alphabet line again without your help.

Extend the activity by having the children form simple words that you spell on the board. Continue by forming simple sentences. Have extra letters ready to assign students if letters appear more than once in a word or sentence. Ask students to come up with their own words to spell too.

Intrapersonal Intelligence

The Three Wishes

The granting of special wishes by magical characters is a theme often seen in both fairy tales and folk tales. In this activity, students will have an opportunity to think about their wishes and what the outcome of those wishes might be.

Read to students the folk tale "The Three Wishes." Here's one version:

> A woodcutter decided not to cut down a giant oak and was granted his next three wishes by a grateful fairy. The foolish man used his first wish by wishing for a tasty sausage. After he told his wife how he got the sausage, she said he was a fool for wasting the wish. She angrily wished that the sausage was stuck to his nose, and it happened! Frantically, the woodcutter and his wife pulled and pulled at the sausage, but try as hard as they could, the sausage was stuck to his nose. The poor woodcutter had to use his last wish to get the sausage off his nose.

After sharing the folk tale, ask students to think about what they might wish for if a fairy granted them three wishes. Give each student a copy of page 22, **The Three Wishes** worksheet. Have students print their wishes on the lines. Encourage them to think about the consequences of their wishes. Provide students with crayons or colored markers and have them draw a picture of themselves after they had all of their wishes granted.

page 22

Naturalist Intelligence

A Tree Book

Create a Tree Book with your students by studying nature over the school year. Create a simple book by cutting large sheets of white construction paper into fourths and stapling the pages together for each student. Give the students blank books and have them write in tree words and draw pictures of what they have observed. Pages can be added as the project continues.

Choose a nearby tree and visit it with your class approximately twice a month to observe changes. Some questions to ask your class:

- What color are the leaves?
- What color is the bark?
- Are there any buds or flowers on the tree?
- What animals are living in or near the tree?
- What bugs live on the tree?
- What is on the ground near the tree?
- Are there any broken branches?
- Has it rained or snowed on the tree recently?
- Is the tree taller or shorter than the trees around it?
- Can you "hug" the tree by stretching your arms around the trunk?
- What kinds of sounds does the tree make?
- How does the tree smell?

The book could be divided into seasons if desired. Write words on the board for students to copy onto their pages, such as *fall, leaves, squirrel, snow,* etc. And have them give their book a title and an author credit.

The Earth Is Painted Green, edited by Barbara Brenner (Scholastic, 1994), has a section of tree poems to read to your students. *One Small Square: Backyard,* by Donal M. Silver (1995 W.H. Freeman), can help your students with their observation skills.

Extend the activity by creating leaf covers for your books. Obtain leaves from the tree and make prints as instructed below.

1. Create a surface to work on by placing old newspaper on tables.

2. Paint one side of a leaf with poster paint.

3. Place the leaf paint-side-down on the piece of paper that will be the cover of the book. Press down firmly with your hand.

4. Remove the leaf and repeat to make a second impression.

5. Allow the cover to dry and then staple to the pages of the book.

6. Leaf imprints can also be made by placing a leaf under a sheet of paper and rubbing with crayon until the leaf's image appears. The leaf shapes can then be cut out with scissors.

Note: The cut-out leaf imprints can be used for bulletin board displays, as name tags, or as gift tags.

A Natural Alphabet

Let children enjoy the forms of nature as they learn the shapes of letters. Gather items from nature, poster board, and all-purpose glue. Assign each child a letter and allow them to pick from a collection of natural materials to create their letters. Simply form the letter with glue on poster board and attach any of the following materials:

pumpkin seeds

twigs and stems

dried leaves and flowers

dried lentils, split peas, and other beans

pearl barley

dried berries

straw

raffia and twine

shells

After all the letters have been made, hang them up in the classroom to create a natural alphabet.

Kindergarten Postcard

Cut out the postcard. Draw a picture on the blank side.
Turn it over and print a message to a classmate on the
left side. Sign your name. Print a classmate's name on the
right side. Then draw in the stamp and mail the postcard.

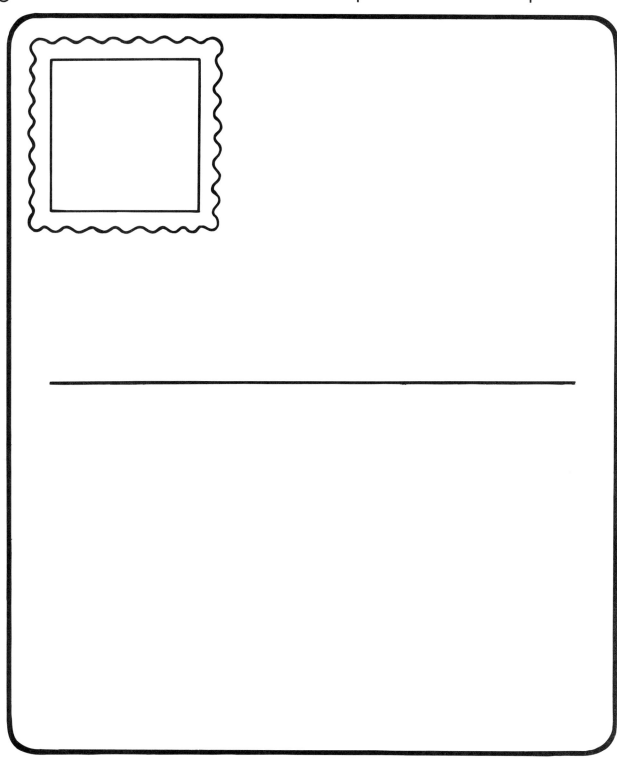

LANGUAGE ARTS
Verbal-Linguistic Intelligence

Name_____

All by Myself

Make a book about things that you can do all by yourself. Complete the sentence on each page. Draw pictures to match your words on the back of the page. Cut the pages on the lines. Then staple the pages together to make a book.

I can _____
all by myself.

I can _____
all by myself.

Make a Match

Match the sea animals to the correct number word.

one

two

three

four

five

six

seven

eight

nine

ten

LANGUAGE ARTS
Logical Mathematical Intelligence

The Three Wishes

Write your three wishes.

My first wish is for

_____.

My second wish is for

_____.

My third wish is for

_____.

On the back of the paper, draw a picture of yourself after your wishes have been granted.

Verbal-Linguistic Intelligence

The Two Cats of Kilkenny

Learning to peacefully resolve a conflict is an important social skill for young children. In this activity, students will examine different options as they help to resolve a conflict between two nursery rhyme characters. First read the following nursery rhyme to your class.

There Were Once Two Cats of Kilkenny

There were once two cats of Kilkenny,

Each thought there was one cat too many;

So they fought and they fit,

And they scratched and they bit,

Till, excepting their nails,

And the tips of their tails,

Instead of two cats, there weren't any.

Explain to your students that the two cats fought with each other because they did not like sharing the neighborhood. The two cats fought until there was nothing left of either of them. Point out that fighting did not get either of the cats what they wanted. So fighting did not help to fix the problem.

Ask your students to think about what the cats could do instead of fighting. Offer students the following suggestions to consider: 1) get to know each other to see if they could share the neighborhood as friends, 2) split the neighborhood up so that each cat had his own half of Kilkenny, or 3) have the cats take turns being in the neighborhood of Kilkenny.

Have students vote on which idea they think might work best for the cats. Ask students to draw a picture of the happy cats of Kilkenny.

I Heard You Say

In this activity, students will play a communication game to experience the fun and confusion that can follow oral messages.

Have students sit in small groups (8 to 10 children per group) in a circle on the floor. Ask one child to start the game by making up a sentence, such as "I went to the circus with my mother and little brother last week." Tell the student not to say the sentence aloud. Ask the student instead to whisper the sentence to the student who is seated directly to his or her right.

Tell students to cup their hands around their mouths as they whisper the message into the next student's ear, so that no one else in the circle will be able to hear the message. Then have each student whisper the same message

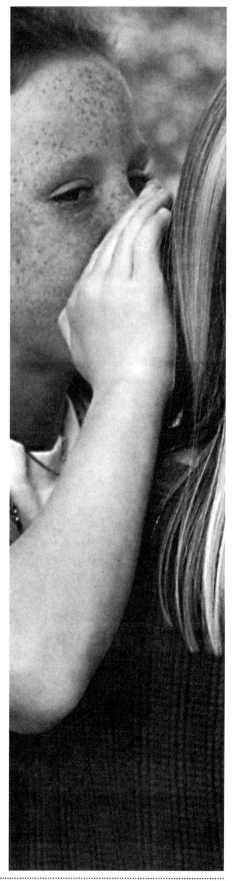

to the student to the right until everyone in the circle has heard the message.

When all the students in the group have had the message whispered to them, the last student to hear the message should speak the message out loud. Students may be surprised to find that the message has changed from person to person. Encourage students to explain how the words and content could change from one person to the next.

Have each student in the group take a turn starting a message and ending one around the circle.

Logical-Mathematical Intelligence

Community Helpers

Illustrate how community helpers effect our lives by making a class chart using the headings below. Get input from the children to fill out the chart.

Community Helpers	What do they do?	Whom do they help?	How do they help?
Mail Carriers	bring our mail	us	We can receive mail from all over the world.
Police Officers	arrest bad guys	us	They keep us safe.
Nurses	give us shots	us	They keep us well.
Trash Carriers	take our trash	us	They help us keep our homes clean.

Discuss with the children the pattern and relationships developed between community helpers and the people they help—us. Then discuss how we could help make community helpers' jobs easier. Ask students if they would like to be a community helper whey they get older.

Bodily-Kinesthetic Intelligence

Where I Live Chant

Teach the children the following chant so that they learn the relationships between home, city, state, and country. Invite the children to stand up and clap to the beat!

Where I Live

I know my address. (Clap to the beat.)

It's home I love best.

I live at: _____. (Child whispers number and street name.)

I live in a city.

It's really quite pretty.

I live in: _____ .(Child says name of city.)

I live in a state

That's really quite great.

It's name is: _____. (Child loudly declares name of state.)

I live in a country

Where people are born free.

It's name is: _____.(Child shouts name of country.)

I know where I live.

I know who I am.

I am _____. (Child flings out arms and shouts his or her

name.) and I am HERE! (Child points dramatically to the floor.)

Dress for the Weather Game

Gather two piles of winter clothes such as boots, mittens, scarves, hats. Divide the children into two teams. Have the teams form two single lines, one in front of each pile of clothes.

When you call out "cold hands," the first two children in line race to put on the mittens. Once the mittens are on, they run to the end of the line. Then call out "wet feet," and the next two children race to put on the boots. Once the boots are on, they run to the end of the line. Continue to call out various cold body parts until the clothes are used up. Then, reverse the process. When you call out "hot head," the children with the hats run to the front of the lines, take off the hats, and return to the line. Call out "dry feet!" The children with the boots run to the front, take off the boots, and return to the line.

This game can also be played as a Dress for Summer game. Simply change the piles of clothes to big, old bathing suits, towels, flippers, etc. Call out things like, "What should I wear to swim in?" or "Need to dry off!"

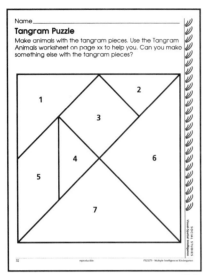

page 32

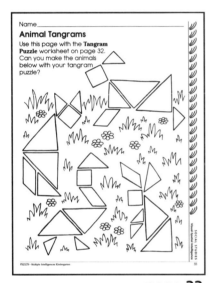

page 33

Visual-Spatial Intelligence

Tangrams

Explain to your students that a tangram is an ancient Chinese puzzle. It is a square cut into seven standard pieces. Each piece is called a tan. All seven tans must be used to form a picture. The pieces must touch but not overlap. Tangrams are used to tell stories in China. The tans are arranged to look like the shape of the characters in the tale.

Have your students do the activities on the **Tangram Puzzle** and **Animal Tangrams** worksheets, found on page 32 and 33. This activity can be done with students paired. Encourage your students to make their own characters with the tangram to illustrate stories.

A Home for Me and You

Homes come in a variety of sizes and shapes, and they are made from many different kinds of materials. In this activity, students will investigate different kinds of homes.

Provide students with photographs, drawings, or magazine cut-outs of different types of homes (single family homes, apartment buildings, mobile homes, pueblos, tepees, long houses, igloos, thatched roof huts, and houseboats). Ask students which homes they have seen before. Good sources are *The House I Live In: At Home in America,* by Isadore Seltzer (Macmillan, 1992), and *Houses and Homes,* by Ann Morris (Lothrop, Lee and Shepard, 1992).

Ask your students what makes a home a special place. On the blackboard, make a list of rooms that most homes have (kitchen, bedroom, and bathroom). Ask students what other features a home might have, and list their answers on the board. (Some possible answers are a staircase, a fireplace, a living room, a laundry room, a family room, or a backyard.) Tell students that one thing that makes all homes the same is that homes are where families come together.

Provide each student with paper, crayons, or colored markers. Have students design a home of their own. Have them use their imaginations and design exactly what they would want in their fantasy home–both interior and exterior. Encourage students to draw furniture, kitchen appliances, and other necessary household items, as well as people and landscaping.

Easy Puzzle

On a large poster board, draw the outline of your state with black marker. Cut the state out, and then cut it into several jigsaw pieces. Children can put the puzzle together and learn the shape of their state.

Build a Community

After studying the community, have the children build their own communities. Give each child half a sheet of tag board. Tell the children to figure out which buildings they want in their communities—a hospital, supermarket, post office? Have the children draw x's on the tag board that suggest where they want their buildings. Children can paint empty milk cartons (saved from the cafeteria) for the buildings. Have them staple the tops of the cartons back together to make roofs. Then have them glue the bottom of the milk cartons to the tag board base. Children can use markers or crayons to draw roads between the buildings. They can paint or draw grass. They can use construction paper scraps to make lakes or parks. Have the children name their cities and make "Welcome to ____" signs. Ask the children to decide what makes each city so special. Have them explain why a person would want to live there.

Musical Intelligence

Mural of America

Teach children to sing "America, the Beautiful." This song lends itself to a big book beautifully! Print the text across the bottom of a long piece of white butcher paper.

Discuss with the children what kinds of pictures they will need to paint so that the pictures match the words. Have them paint a mural across the top part of the butcher paper. One portion could be purple mountains; one could be amber waves of grain. Have the children paint the ocean on the extreme left and right of the butcher paper mural. Label the left side Pacific and the right side Atlantic.

Showing What You Feel

Children often have difficulty putting their feelings into words. Modifying this simple song and accompanying body gestures may help your students explore the feelings they experience in a fun and active way.

If You're Happy and You Know It

If you're happy and you know it

Clap your hands!

If you're happy and you know it

Clap your hands!

If you're happy and you know it,

And you really want to show it,

If you're happy and you know it,

Clap your hands!

Have students sing the song with you and clap their hands. Tell students that the words of the song can be changed to tell about other kinds of feelings, such as mad, sad, or scared. Write the words of the song on the board. Explain that the word *happy* and the phrase *clap your hands* can be substituted for other feelings and action words. Demonstrate how a new version of the song can be made by substituting these words.

If you're mad and you know it, pound your fists.

(Bang a fist into the palm of other hand.)

OR

If you're sad and you know it, wipe your tears.

(Pretend to wipe tears from your eyes.)

OR

If you're scared and you know it, shake and shiver.

(Jump up and down.)

Interpersonal Intelligence

I'm in a Family

In this activity, students will learn about the different types of families and the special gift family members give to each other.

Show students a variety of family pictures—from those found in picture books to families portrayed in magazines. Point out pictures that show the following:

- a single parent with one or more children
- a two-parent family—a mother and father with one or more children
- two mothers with one or more children
- two fathers with one or more children
- a two-parent family with extended family members (aunts, uncles, grandparents, etc.)
- a family with adopted children

Ask students to discuss how they can tell that the pictures are of families. Ask if the people in the pictures look like they enjoy each other, support each other, and show their love for each other. Explain that people in a family can show their love in many ways—spending time together, talking to each other, reading a story, or helping each other.

Ask students to describe the things that their family members do to show their love for each other. Give each student drawing paper and crayons or colored markers. Have each student draw a picture of his or her family. Help each student write a caption for his or her picture.

Circle Time

About three times a week, gather the children in a circle. Instruct each child to say something that he or she appreciates about someone else in the classroom. A child may start the statement by saying, "I appreciate the way that___." He or she might say, "I appreciate the way that Jane helped me clean up the paint that I spilled." Tell the children to be on the lookout for someone who treated them with kindness and thoughtfulness. It takes practice, but doing this sets the tone for a gentle classroom.

Pizza Parlor

Read *Little Nino's Pizzeria,* by Karen Barbour (Harcourt Brace Jovanovich, 1990). Set up a dramatic play center with modeling clay, cookie sheets, aprons, pads of paper, pens, a play cash register, and utensils. Invite the children to create their own pizzeria. Children can be cooks, waiters, or customers. You might even have a play phone for take-out orders. Using chart paper, make a menu board with prices. Children will practice reading and writing when ordering and can even practice math if you make the price list appropriate to their skill levels.

 Intrapersonal Intelligence

A Moment in Time

Pictures of people, places, and things from long ago help children begin to grasp the concept of history. In this activity, students will be asked to make a time capsule.

Gather a few items from an earlier period in history (clothing, an LP, a video of a 1960s television program, or photographs from early in the century). Allow students to look at the pictures and hear the sounds of what life was like long before they were born. Encourage students to think about the people you show them and discuss how life was different then.

Tell students that they are going to share some things about themselves with people in the future by building their own time capsules. Explain that each

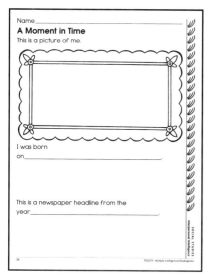

page 34

student's time capsule will be a special package of personal items that tells others about their life. The time capsules will include a newspaper headline, a photograph of themselves, and a piece of schoolwork.

Ask each student to bring the following items from home: a photograph of himself or herself, a newspaper headline, and a large plastic or glass jar with a twist-on lid. Have students complete the **A Moment in Time** worksheet on page 34 by writing dates on the lines and gluing on the headline and a photocopy of their picture in the space provided.

They should also draw a picture on a separate piece of paper. Give each student crayons for drawing. Let students draw a picture of something that is special to them or of something that they like to do. Remind students to draw something that they would like to share with people in the future. Then ask students to pick a school activity on paper that they have already completed to add to the capsule.

Provide a water-safe, zip-lock freezer bag for each student. Have each student place the worksheet drawing and schoolwork in the bag, then place the bag into the jar and twist on the lid. Have students take their time capsules home and ask a parent to choose a safe location inside the home to stash it or a place outside where it can be buried.

Naturalist Intelligence

Every Day Is Earth Day

Discuss Earth Day with your class. A simple explanation can be found in *Earth Day*, by Linda Lowry (Carolrhoda, 1991). Other useful titles are *Recycle!* by Gail Gibbons (Little, Brown, 1992), and *50 Simple Things Kids Can Do to Save the Earth*, by John Javna (Andrews and McMeel, 1990). Then ask the children what they can do to help preserve the planet. Explain that everyone must work together to achieve this goal. Write a list on the board of things that can be done, for example:

- · pick up litter
- · conserve water
- · plant a tree
- · collect money for a conservation cause
- · walk or ride a bike instead of driving
- · reuse grocery bags
- · recycle paper at school

Make an Earth Day Helping Hands Mobile to illustrate the cooperative nature of the effort to save the planet. Each child should trace his or her hand on construction paper. The child should write her or his name on the hand and, with your help, what he or she can do to keep the planet clean and green. Hang the paper hands on several coat hangers in the classroom. You might also want to add cut-out construction paper silhouettes of objects from nature such as leaves, flowers, birds, etc., to add to the mobiles.

Recyled Art

Ask children to bring old magazines and junk mail with colorful pictures from home to class for several weeks. The paper should be torn into small scraps approximately one square inch and sorted by color. Put the sorted scraps in used containers or grocery bags with color labels on them. When a good amount has been collected, have children create cooperative works of art. They can create a flag of their country, a scene from nature, or a poster with a slogan such as "Earth Day Is Everyday." First draw the picture or slogan on butcher paper and label the drawing with the colors to be used in the proper places. Let the children glue the scraps of paper to create their artwork and then hang it in the classroom.

Tangram Puzzle

Make animals with the tangram pieces. Use the **Animal Tangrams** worksheet on page 33 to help you. Can you make something else with the tangram pieces?

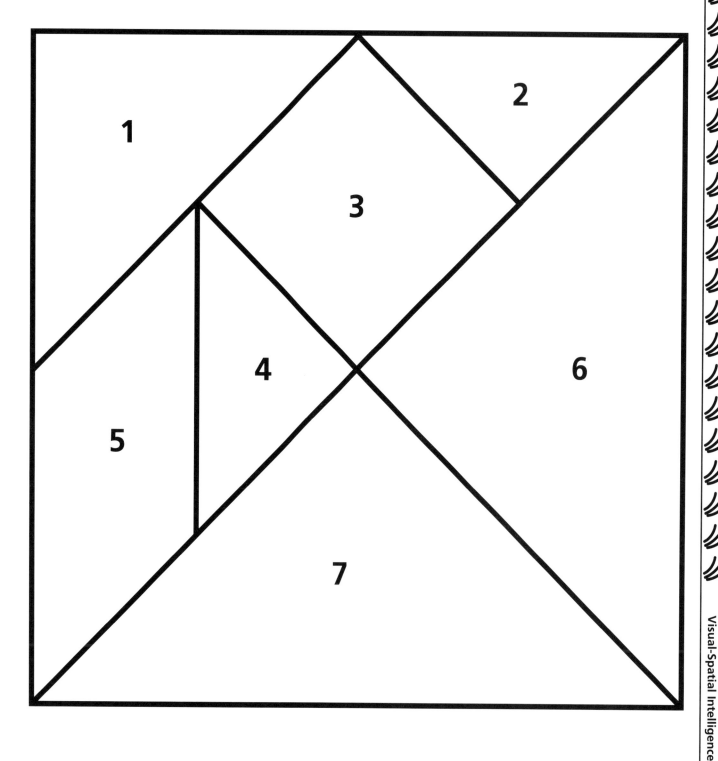

Name_____

Animal Tangrams

Use this page with the **Tangram Puzzle** worksheet on page 32. Can you make the animals below with your tangram puzzle?

Name_____

A Moment in Time

This is a picture of me.

I was born

on_____.

This is a newspaper headline from the

year_____.

reproducible

SOCIAL STUDIES
Intrapersonal Intelligence

Verbal-Linguistic Intelligence

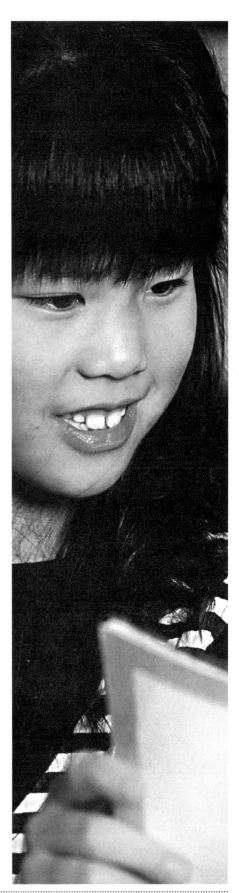

Ordinal Counting

Tell students that another way to count is by using ordinal numbers. In this activity, students will use ordinal numbers to name positions within a series of numbered objects.

Gather five counters (small wooden blocks or toy animals). Place the counters in a row on the floor or on a table. Ask students to help you count the counters using ordinal numbers. Point to the first counter in the row and tell students that this counter is called "first."

Ask a student volunteer to point to the item that would be called "second." Tell students that an item that is counted as "two" can also be called "second." Continue with third and fourth, using the same instructions. Then point to the last item in the row and ask students if they can guess what this item would be called. Some students may suggest "fifth" and others may call out "last." Tell students that both terms are correct. An item that is counted as "five" can also be called "fifth." Items that end a row or series can also be called "last."

To help students grasp the concept of number position, place five carpet squares on the floor. Have a student volunteer stand on the first square. Explain that this position is "first." Ask other volunteers to stand on the remaining squares. Walk behind them calling out their ordinal numbers as you pass. Then put your hand above a student volunteer's head and ask the class if anyone can tell you what ordinal number the student represents. Continue this activity until all five of the ordinal numbers and "last" have been called out correctly.

Calendar Teams

Review the days of the week and months of the year with the class. Then divide the class into teams of approximately three. Each team should have a set of cards with the days of the week and the months written on them–one word on each card. Have each team put the days and months in order. This activity can also be done with a timer to further illustrate the concept of time.

Once the class has learned calendar order, assign a specific day and month to each child. Have each child hold the day or month card up so the class can see it. Then have the class arrange themselves in the correct order.

Logical-Mathematical Intelligence

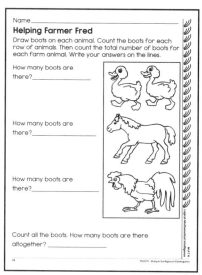

page 44

page 45

Helping Farmer Fred

Tell students that they are going to do a math activity that will help a silly farmer take care of his farm animals. Explain to students that winter is very cold where the farmer lives. So Farmer Fred has decided that he wants all of his animals to wear warm winter boots. The problem is that he is not sure how many boots to buy when he goes to the shoe store. The students will need to help Farmer Fred figure out how many boots he needs to buy.

Write the following information on the board for your students.

Farmer Fred has

2 ducks

1 rooster

1 horse

Pass out the **Helping Farmer Fred** worksheet on page 44. Have students count the animals aloud with you. Ask them if that is the number of boots that Farmer Fred needs. Lead students to see that it is not the correct number. Encourage students to discuss how they can figure out how many winter boots are needed for the farm animals.

Give each student some crayons. Have them draw winter boots on the farm animals. Then have them count the boots on each animal and write the numeral on the line. Then ask them to count the total number of boots and write the number on the line.

Parts and Wholes

This activity will help students expand their understanding of the relationship between parts and wholes. Provide students with scissors, glue, a large manila envelope, and old magazines. Have students look through the magazines for pictures or illustrations that they find interesting. They should cut out a few of their favorite pictures. Then they should glue the pictures to construction paper or tagboard.

Ask students to cut their pictures into five parts. Let students experiment with putting the picture back together. Have students trade their picture puzzles with a classmate. Challenge them to put the parts back together so they can see the whole picture. Remind students to make sure that all of the parts of their pictures are returned to their envelopes so that they can play with their puzzles again.

Pass out a copy of the **Parts and Wholes** worksheet on page 45. Provide pencils and crayons. Students can complete each drawing.

Estimating

Create an activity to teach estimation by filling large jars with a variety of different-sized objects. Erasers, jelly beans, counting toys, pencils, crayons, and other items can be used. Number the jars. Have the students number their answer sheets accordingly and then put their guesses down on paper. Then ask students to count the objects. Switch the objects in the jars with other objects and have the children guess again.

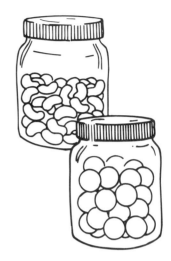

Bodily-Kinesthetic Intelligence

Measuring With My Feet

In this activity, students will be using nonstandard measurements to measure objects in the classroom and on the playground. Measure out a length of string or twine as long as your foot. Explain that this length of string is the exact length of a "teacher foot." Tell students that this nonstandard measurement can be used to measure anything in the classroom, such as a tabletop. Place the "teacher foot" string on a tabletop and measure it. Write the number of "teacher feet" the tabletop measures on the blackboard.

Provide students with a small ball of string or twine. Have each student measure the length of his or her foot with the string. (Tell students to keep their shoes on.) Cut the string for each student so that it is the same length as the student's foot. Remind students that their foot-length string is a "Ryan foot" or an "Ana foot."

Ask students to record the number of "student feet" it takes to measure the items listed on the **Measuring With My Feet** worksheet on page 46. Explain the terms *height, length,* and *width* as students are measuring. Have students compare their measurement findings with each other and discuss why they have different or similar measurements.

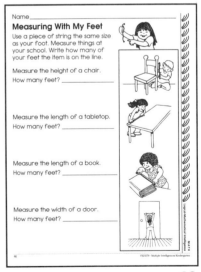

page 46

Count Your Eggs

The game Count Your Eggs is intended to help children understand how numbers can be broken down into groups of tens and ones (for example, 36 is three groups of ten and six ones).

You will need many empty 12-count egg cartons. Cut off the lid and two end egg spaces in each carton. Give each child, or each pair of children, several egg cartons, a small bowl, and access to manipulatives, such as one-inch interlocking cubes, counting bears, or wooden cubes.

Have each child, or each pair of children, scoop up a bowlful of manipulatives. Have the children consider this a "basket of eggs." Next, have the children put each "egg" in an egg space in a carton. When one carton is full, instruct the children to fill another. The children are building groups of ten in the cartons; any extra eggs are left in the basket. When finished, have the children count the cartons and the extra eggs. They might say, "We have 4 cartons of eggs and 2 extra. We have 4 groups of ten and 2 extra. We have 42 eggs."

Feel a Shape

Students use their sense of touch in this activity to discriminate between different shapes. Gather a variety of wooden, rubber, or plastic geometric shapes (circles, squares, triangles, rectangles, diamonds, and ovals). Place one of each shape into several clean, heavy cotton socks. (Drawstring cloth bags can be used in place of socks.) Take each shape out of one sock, one at a time, so students can see the shapes. Ask students to name each shape. Put the shapes back into the sock. Ask several student volunteers to come forward and put a hand into a sock.

Ask the students to select one shape and to describe what they feel with their fingers. Encourage them to use descriptive words, such as *round, curved, pointy,* or *corners,* as they feel the shape with their fingers. Have the watching students guess what the shape might be from the oral clues. After the students have described the shape, ask them to name the shape and remove the shape from the sock. Tell all the students to check their guesses against what the shape looks like.

Have students take turns feeling the shapes with their fingers, describing the shape's attributes, and naming the geometric shapes.

Provide drawing paper and crayons for students to draw the shapes they felt with their fingers. Encourage them to label each shape.

Visual-Spatial Intelligence

Box City

The architecture in cities is made up of combinations of shapes and designs. In this activity, students will use a variety of shapes to create a city. Gather a wide assortment of cardboard boxes, cartons, and paper tubes. Ask your students to bring in clean boxes and cartons from home. Lightweight cardboard such as the kind used for cereal and cracker boxes works well, as it can be cut easily. Also collect tubes used for wrapping paper, paper towels and toilet tissue, small boxes for jewelry, shoe boxes, and various sizes of gift boxes. Provide each student with safety scissors, a small bottle of glue, and a flat piece of sturdy cardboard to serve as a base for the city.

Show students a few photographs of a city and its skyline. Make sure the scenes include a variety of tall, short, wide, narrow, rectangular, and circular

buildings, domes, and towers. Tell students they will be using the boxes to design a city of their own. Explain that architects and builders put a great deal of mathematical thinking into the buildings they make.

Encourage students to carefully select the boxes, tubes, and cartons they will use to build their city. Ask them to think about how wide, tall or strong they would like the buildings to be. Tell students that they can cut and combine the boxes and tubes to form their buildings, or glue them as they are to the cardboard base. They can also include roads and sidewalks in their creations.

After students have completed their cities and the glue is dry, provide tempera paint and paintbrushes so they can paint and add details to their buildings. To add a little sparkle to the city, allow students to sprinkle some salt in the paint. The salt will sparkle in the light when it dries.

Small, Medium, and Large

In this activity, students will be sorting various objects in three different sizes—small, medium, and large. A good way to get students prepared for this activity is to share the story of "Goldilocks and the Three Bears." In the story, Papa Bear uses large things, Mama Bear uses medium-sized things, and Baby Bear uses small things.

Gather a variety of objects, such as buttons, cups, spools, shells, toy cars, shoes, and boxes and place them on a table. Make sure each category has at least one small, one medium, and one large object.

Print the words small, medium, and large on three different-colored large sheets of construction paper. Place the paper on the table with the different-sized objects. Tell students that they will sort the objects by size. Ask them to place objects that are small on the paper with the word *small*, and so on.

Reinforce the concepts with the **Small, Medium, and Large** worksheet on page 47.

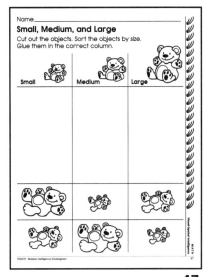

page 47

Symmetry

Teach the children that when things are symmetrical, they can be divided along their line of symmetry into two pieces that are exactly alike. First cut a length of string about two feet long. Invite a volunteer to the front of the room. Hold the string from the child's forehead, down the nose, to the end of the chin. (While faces are not exactly alike on both sides, they're close enough for this lesson.) Discuss with the children whether the volunteer's face is the same on both sides. Could we put half of John's face together with half of Xavier's face and get a match?

Then hold the string across the volunteer's face at the nose with the string stretching from ear to ear. Ask the children if both halves of the face are the same. Point out that one half of the face has the mouth, chin, and nostrils, and the other half has the forehead, eyes, and eyebrows. Are both halves the same? Explain that where something is divided determines symmetry.

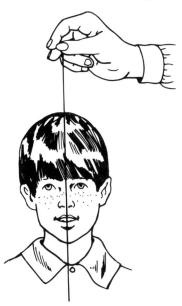

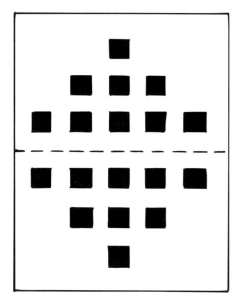

Group the children into pairs. Give each pair a 12-by-18-inch piece of black construction paper and some pattern blocks. Fold the paper in half so that there is a crease down the middle. Open the paper. Have the children build a design with the pattern blocks on the paper, with the crease being the line of symmetry. The children in each pair will have to work closely together, discussing each block as they put it down, so that both sides will be the same. You might have them take turns—one child puts down a block, then the other child puts down the same block.

To make this easier in the beginning, limit the number of blocks the children can use in their designs. Start with six blocks (three on each side) and increase the number as they get the hang of it.

Musical Intelligence

The Beat of a Different Drummer

Use a tom-tom drum to teach children to count and develop their listening and rhythm skills. Tap out numbers for children to count. Then have the children say the number and then clap the number. Increase your speed as children become accustomed to the activity. Try doing simple addition problems also. For example, 2 + 2 would be two taps, then say "plus," then tap two more times. Have the children say the answer and then clap the answer.

Rhyming With Numbers

These playful verses help children learn about numbers, counting, and rhythm in fun and meaningful ways. First write the rhyme "One, Two, Buckle My Shoe" on the blackboard.

One, Two, Buckle My Shoe

One, two, buckle my shoe;

Three, four, shut the door;

Five, six, pick up sticks;

Seven, eight, lay them straight;

Nine, ten, a big fat hen.

Point out to your students that the last word in each line rhymes with a number (shoe/two, door/four, etc.). Tell students that they can write a new counting rhyme by changing the rhyming phrase in each line. Point to the first line and ask students to think about another phrase that would rhyme with "One, two." Offer the following examples to give them inspiration.

One, two, I like blue

Or

One, two, Who are you?

Write one or more of their responses on a sentence strip and tape it to the board above the appropriate line of the rhyme. Continue with each line of the rhyme until the new counting rhyme is complete. Have students chant the new rhyme together.

Provide students with drawing paper and crayons. Ask them to illustrate their favorite phrase from the rhyme. Tell students to make the numerals (1, 2, etc.) and then make a drawing of the rhyming phrase.

Cake for Everyone

Young children learn about dividing long before they encounter it in math class. In this activity, students will be deciding how to slice a paper cake into equal pieces.

Draw a large circle on construction paper or chart paper. Cut out the circle and decorate it to look like a pretend cake. Show students the paper cake. Tell them that they must figure out how to cut the cake so that everyone at a pretend party will receive the same size piece.

Tell students that the cake will need to be cut for four people. Everyone will want to have the same size piece of cake. Ask students to think about how they could cut the cake so that each of the four pieces would be the same size.

Use a thick, black marker to demonstrate that two straight lines crossing the cake in the middle will divide it into four equal pieces. Use a pair of scissors to cut along the dark lines. Explain that you have divided a whole cake into four equal pieces to make four servings of dessert. Have students put the four triangular pieces back together again to see how the parts fit together to form a whole cake.

Give each student a six-inch construction-paper circle, a pencil, and a pair of safety scissors. Tell students that they need to divide a pie for eight people. Have students use a pencil to divide the "pie" into equal pieces. (Encourage the use of "trial and error" to successfully complete this exercise.) Remind students to make sure that each piece of pie is the same size or "equal" to the other pieces of pie. When students have successfully divided their pies, let them cut along the pencil lines to make the individual pieces of pie.

Intrapersonal Intelligence

1	
2	
3	X X X X
4	
5	
6	X X X
7	
8	X X X X
9	
10	

Name Graph

Create a bar graph of the number of letters in students' names. First have each child write his or her name on paper. Ask them to count the number of letters in their name and write the number under their name. Create the graph by writing the numbers 1 through 10 on the left side of a rectangle and drawing lines to make horizontal rows.

Each child should go up to the chart and put a check mark next to the number that indicates how many letters in his or her name. When all the students have done this, discuss the chart. Ask students which numbers have the most checks and the least. Brainstorm on other topics that can be charted, such as:

·how many children are wearing sneakers or shoes

·blue, green, and brown eyes

·favorite colors, foods, or pets

Happy Birthday Bulletin Board

This birthday activity develops your students' self-expression while reviewing picture graphs. During the first weeks of school, have your students help create a birthday bulletin board for your classroom. List the names of the twelve months along the left side of a bulletin board. Put lines on the bulletin board at least 5 inches apart. Give each student a 5-by-5-inch sheet of paper. Have the students paint or color a portrait of themselves. Have them write their name and birthday under their portrait. Help the students pin or staple their portraits on the graph. After the graph is completed, have the class examine it. Ask the students questions such as these: *Which month has the most birthdays? How many students have birthdays in December? How many more birthdays are in May than in July?*

Naturalist Intelligence

Seed Patterns

Stimulate naturalist intelligence by having students discover unique patterns in fruits and vegetables. You will need a knife and a variety of fruits and vegetables that contain seeds or pits, such as banana, apple, kiwi, orange, cucumber, strawberry, tomato, zucchini, plum, or avocado. Cut open one of the fruits or vegetables and pass it around for students to examine. Ask students these questions: *How many seeds are there? What patterns in the seeds do you find? What part do we eat?* Cut the same item in a different way. Have students examine this pattern. Challenge students to discern if the pattern is the same or different. Repeat the activity with other fruits and vegetables and have the children draw some of the patterns.

Weather Patterns

Keep track of weather over a period of weeks with your class. Help them collect data about precipitation, type of cloud cover, temperature, and wind speed and direction. Data can be a combination of observation, measurement, and use of published or broadcast weather reports. Keep track of information on a large weather chart. Illustrate each weather concept with a drawing or photo.

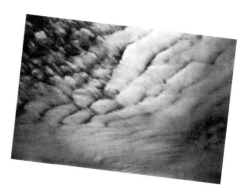

At the end of the time period, study the data with students. Count the number of days of precipitation, clouds, and sun. List the types of cloud formations. Discuss the different wind speeds and directions. Look for averages, and changes such as steady drops in temperature or an increase in sunny days.

Helping Farmer Fred

Draw boots on each animal. Count the boots for each row of animals. Then count the total number of boots for each animal. Write your answers on the lines.

How many boots are

there?_____

How many boots are

there?_____

How many boots are

there?_____

Count all the boots. How many boots are there

altogether? _____

Logical-Mathematical Intelligence

MATH

Parts and Wholes

Complete each picture by drawing the missing piece.

MATH

Logical-Mathematical Intelligence

Measuring With My Feet

Use a piece of string the same size as your foot. Measure things at your school. Write how many of your feet the item is on the line.

Measure the height of a chair.

How many feet? _____

Measure the length of a tabletop.

How many feet? _____

Measure the length of a book.

How many feet? _____

Measure the width of a door.

How many feet? _____

Bodily-Kinesthetic Intelligence

MATH

Name_____

Small, Medium, and Large

Cut out the objects. Sort the objects by size.
Glue them in the correct column.

Small	Medium	Large

Verbal-Linguistic Intelligence

The Wind

Read to your class the picture book *The Air Around Us,* by Eleonore Schmid (North-South Books, 1992). Then read the poem "The Wind," by Robert Louis Stevenson to your students. If it is a windy day, open the windows a bit. Or supply a recording of the wind. For the second reading of the poem, ask your students to say the two chorus lines that come at the end of each verse. If this is too difficult, have half the class say one line and half say the other line. While you are reading the verses, have the children make the soft sound of the wind by blowing air out of their mouths.

The Wind

I saw you toss the kites on high

And blow the birds about the sky;

And all around I heard you pass,

Like ladies' skirts across the grass–

    O wind, a-blowing all day long,

    O wind, that sings so loud a song!

I saw the different things you did,

But always you yourself you hid.

I felt you push, I heard you call,

I could not see yourself at all–

    O wind, a-blowing all day long,

    O wind, that sings so loud a song!

O you that are so strong and cold,

O blower, are you young or old?

Are you a beast of field and tree,

Or just a stronger child than me?

    O wind, a-blowing all day long,

    O wind, that sings so loud a song!

Logical-Mathematical Intelligence

Living Things/Nonliving Things

Talk to the children about the differences between living and nonliving things. Teach the children that living things need food, water, and air to live. Do the following experiment to find out what happens when living things don't get what they need.

Plant seven lima bean seeds in seven different cups. Label the cups as follows:

    Cup #1—Food, Water, and Air

    Cup #2—Food and Water Only

    Cup #3—Food and Air Only

    Cup #4—Food Only

    Cup #5—Water and Air Only

    Cup #6—Water Only

    Cup #7—Air Only

Teach the children that plants get food from the soil, but they also make food from sunlight (photosynthesis). Give each plant the same start by planting the seeds in potting soil. Give plant #1 the good life—sunshine, water, and air. Give plant #2 sunshine and water, but keep it in a plastic baggy. Give plant #3 sunlight and air, but no water. Give plant #4 sunshine, but keep it in a plastic baggy with no water. Give plant #5 water and air, but no sunlight. Give plant #6 water, but keep it in a plastic baggy and give it no sunlight. Give plant #7 air, but no sunshine and no water.

Have the children help you figure out where in the room the plants can go in order to perform the experiment. Assign seven children to be "plant managers," one for each plant. These children are in charge of giving each plant what is required for the experiment.

Make a large chart titled "Plant Progress," and have the children as a whole report what is happening to each plant. Write the information down on the chart twice a week. Children will begin to prove and conclude that living things need food, water, and air.

Animals, Animals Everywhere

In this activity, students will classify animals by where they live and how they get around. Create three poster collages of scenes where animals can be found. Gather three large pieces of cardboard and photographs from old magazines of sky scenes, underwater scenes, and forest, desert, and grassland scenes. (Old *National Geographic* magazines would be a good source for pictures.) Write *air, water,* and *land* on each of the pieces of cardboard. Paste the pictures on the cardboard according to the type of scene—sky (air), underwater (water), forest, desert, and grassland (land).

Place the posters on the ledge of the blackboard so that all students can easily see them. Tell students that these are the three places where animals can be found. Ask students to look at the environments shown on the three posters and tell you where they could find the following animals:

- a puppy
- a bird
- a fish
- a lion
- a seal
- a cat
- a duck
- a hawk

Explain that some animals can spend time in one, two, or even all three environments (a duck can fly, swim, and walk), but that others stay in only one (a cat is a land animal, and a fish cannot live out of water).

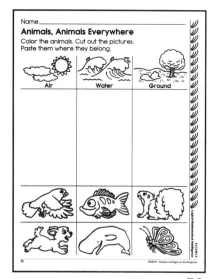

page 56

Give each student a copy of the **Animals, Animals Everywhere** worksheet on page 56, some crayons, and a pair of safety scissors. Tell students to color and cut out the pictures of the animals. Then ask students to think about where they might find each animal—in the air, under the water, or on the ground. Have students paste the animals to the appropriate section on the page.

Bodily-Kinesthetic Intelligence

Erosion

Read *The Sun, the Wind, and the Rain,* by Lisa W. Peters (Henry Holt, 1990). Have the students study rocks and sand. How do they compare? With the help of magnifying glasses, the children may discover that sand is little, tiny rocks. Ask them to guess how they got so small. Then introduce the concept of erosion, the gradual wearing away or deterioration of something.

Set up an experiment where the children can learn how rocks become sand. Fill a big container with a pile of rocks and sand. Have the children make a mountain with the rocks and sand. Ask a few children to blow on the mountain as hard as they can. (They should all face the same direction, and

keep the other children away.) Have the children discuss what happened. Elicit discussion that relates the blowing of air to the wind outside.

Next, fill a watering can with water. Have the children pour water over the mountain. Have them discuss what happens to the mountain. Let a few children take turns dropping a rock onto a rock—relate this to waves picking up rocks and dashing them against other rocks. Have a few other children rub rocks with sandpaper. Teach the children that over millions of years this constant barrage of moving water and blowing wind has caused (and continues to cause) the breakdown of mountains and rocks into sand—erosion!

Use Your Nose

In this activity, students will use their sense of smell to help them identify scents and match them to the correct item. You'll need the following: six clean small, unbreakable containers (such as plastic film cases or spice containers), six large cotton balls, and a variety of items that produce a strong odor (such as an orange, a lemon, vanilla, mint leaves, a rose, garlic, coffee, a pine bough).

Squeeze the juice from the fruits or mash the leaves, needles, or petals of the plants so that the odors from these items can be absorbed by the cotton balls. Place each of the items in one of the containers with a cotton ball and tighten the lid securely. Allow the items to stay in their containers overnight, so that the cotton balls can absorb as much of the odors as possible. Before beginning the activity, empty the container of any residual juice or organic material, so that only the saturated cotton ball is left in the container.

Provide a picture or drawing of each item on index cards. Have students match each picture with its "smell."

Visual-Spatial Intelligence

Petal Power

Read *The Reason for a Flower,* by Ruth Heller (Putnam, 1983). Hang up a poster of a flower, such as Georgia O'Keeffe's "Red Poppy," and scrutinize and discuss it. Have the children collect flowers and spread them all over the tables. Provide magnifying glasses and allow the children time to look at the flowers closely. Allow them to take them apart and look at each piece. Have them identify the parts of a flower: the petal, the leaf, and the stem.

Next, give each child a piece of 9-by-12-inch white construction paper. Ask each child to choose a flower. With a black, permanent, fine-line marker, have each child draw the flower (nice and big!). Tell the children to pay close attention to detail and draw what they see. Next, allow the children to paint their pictures with watercolor paints and display them in the classroom.

Musical Intelligence

Fun From Head to Toe

Students will have fun exploring the parts of the body through music, song, and movement. In this activity, students will move in time with the rhythm of a song as they locate body parts and sing "Head, Shoulders, Knees, and Toes."

Have students stand in a circle. Tell them that they are going to sing a fun song that some of them may have heard before. Explain to students that as they are singing they should move their fingers to the body part being named. Sing the song through once for your students and demonstrate the song's movements by touching your head, shoulders, knees, and toes as you sing the appropriate words. Then encourage students to sing and move along with you.

Head, Shoulders, Knees, and Toes

Head, shoulders, knees, and toes—

knees and toes.

Head, shoulders, knees, and toes—

knees and toes.

Eyes and ears and mouth and nose,

Head, shoulders, knees, and toes—

knees and toes.

As students learn the tune, and the sequence of body parts, change the word order and speed of the song. These changes will add to the fun and increase the need for students to watch and listen carefully.

Interpersonal Intelligence

Lessons From a Tree

Read *The Giving Tree,* by Shel Silverstein (HarperCollins, 1964), to your students. Discuss the concept of giving and generosity. Ask students what else nature gives to us and what we can give to nature. Discuss the concept of "Mother Nature" with your students.

Then explain the concept of a "family tree" with the class. Have the students draw family trees illustrating their family members. Discuss what family members do for your students and what they can do for their families.

Create a class tree on a bulletin board using leaves with students' names written on them. (See the method of making leaf prints in The Tree Book activity on page 17.) Make leaves for other people at school who help your class, such as the principal, substitute teachers, maintenance workers, and so on. Along the branches write words that tell how all the members of the class help each other, such as *share, give directions, teach, clean up,* etc.

Intrapersonal Intelligence

My, How You Have Grown!

Children are often so anxious to get bigger that they fail to recognize how much they have already grown. In this activity, students will review how much they have grown and changed.

Gather a series of photographs that show the normal cycle of growth for children—from infant to toddler to preschooler to kindergartner. Ask students to bring to class photographs of themselves as babies and toddlers, along with a current picture. Show the photographs of each student in chronological order on a bulletin board display titled *We Have Really Grown!* Lead students in a discussion of the differences they see between the photographs.

Naturalist Intelligence

Rock Rangers

In this activity, students will collect rocks. As they study the rocks, students will begin to appreciate the rocks for their unique colors, textures, and sizes.

Ask students if they have ever collected rocks during a walk, a camping trip, or during another kind of outdoor adventure. Ask them to bring a few of their favorite rocks to the classroom to share. Prepare a special table or area in the classroom for students to display their collections. Supply magnifying glasses so that students can carefully observe and study these amazing objects of nature.

Have students sit in small groups. Ask students who brought rocks to share to introduce their rock collections to their group. Encourage the groups to examine the rocks as you tell them the following information about rocks:

- Rocks and rock material cover the entire surface of the earth.
- The different colors, shadings, and markings on a rock provide information about the minerals that make up that rock.
- Minerals have different crystal patterns and form rocks in a variety of shapes and sizes.
- Rocks with many colored layers are called sedimentary rocks.
- Rocks formed from sand are called sandstone.
- Rocks formed from clay are called shale.
- Rocks formed from small pebbles and hardened sand are called conglomerate rocks.

Encourage students to study the rocks to discover their unique shape, texture, and color. Ask students to think about how the rocks they have studied are like people. Tell them that people also have their own shape, texture, and color. Just like the rocks they examined, each person is special because of his or her unique characteristics. When we stop to take a closer look at someone, we get to see what is special about them.

Bug Barn

Help students build a special viewing place for the small bugs and crawly things they find in the great outdoors. You will need several clean, empty oatmeal containers, some wire screening, duct tape, and scissors. Use a pair of scissors to cut two large windows into each oatmeal container. Cut pieces of wire screening about one inch larger than each of the windows. Center the screening over the windows, with about half an inch of overlay on each side. Use the duct tape to secure the screening in place. Make sure the entire

border of the screening has been securely taped to the container. Fill the container with moist dirt, grass clippings, and a few small twigs. When the environment is ready, add ladybugs, beetles, or other safe insects for students to observe and place the lid on the container.

To collect the insects, have students walk to a nearby park, garden, or field area. Explain that more than half of all the living creatures on Earth are insects. Most insects are arthropods. This means that they have bodies that are divided into three sections: the head, the thorax, and the abdomen. Most insects have six legs. Many of these creatures also have a pair of feelers or antennae, and a pair of wings. Ladybugs are excellent examples of arthropods for students to study in the bug barns. Set magnifying glasses near the bug barn display area so students can observe the bugs very closely.

Have students collect leaves, grasses, and water for the insects while they are guests in your classroom. Tell students that you can keep bugs in the classroom for observation for three to four days. After that the insects must be released outside to live their lives naturally.

After students have had an opportunity to examine and study the bugs, provide each student with a copy of the **Bug Barn** worksheet on page 57. Have students color and cut out the bug cards. Students can separate into pairs and play a matching game with their bug cards. Tell the pairs that the student who matches the most bug pictures in each group wins the game. Allow students to play several games so that each student will have the opportunity to win.

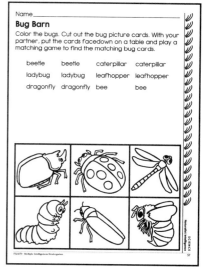

page 57

Clean Up Inside and Out

To help your students see how much paper is used everyday in class, put all paper to be thrown away into a large trash can and ask the maintenance department in your school not to throw it away. At the end of the week have the class see how much paper was used. After the class has done the **Don't Litter** worksheet on page 58, have them use the back of the worksheet for another activity.

page 58

Animals, Animals Everywhere

Color the animals. Cut out the pictures.
Paste them where they belong.

Air	Water	Ground

reproducible
FS23279 · Multiple Intelligences Kindergarten

SCIENCE

Logical-Mathematical Intelligence

Bug Barn

Color the bugs. Cut out the bug picture cards. With your partner, put the cards facedown on a table and play a matching game to find the matching bug cards.

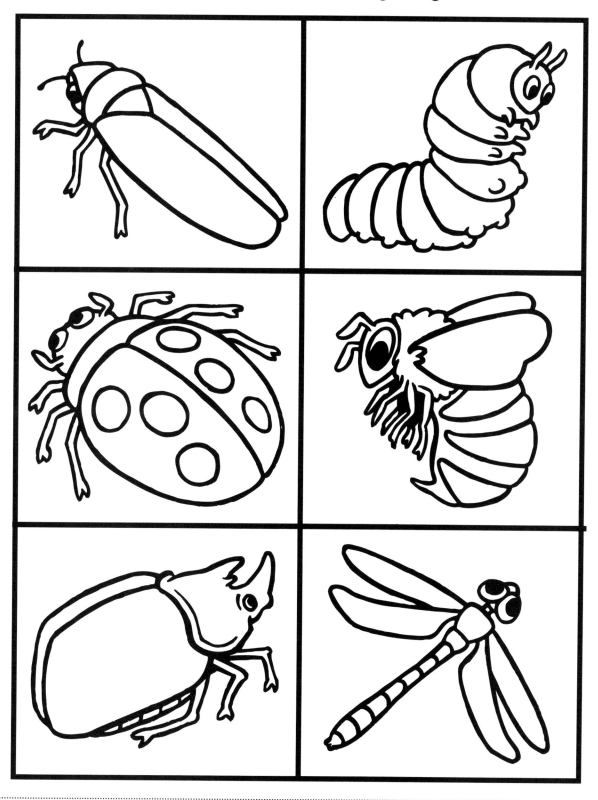

reproducible

SCIENCE
Naturalist Intelligence

Name_____

Don't Litter

Color the picture of the seashore. Then put a big X on all the trash that should go in the trash can. There are five pieces of trash.

reproducible FS23279 · Multiple Intelligences Kindergarten

SCIENCE
Naturalist Intelligence

Verbal-Linguistic Intelligence

What Do You Think?

Nurture your students' sensitivity to art by displaying Norman Rockwell illustrations(calendars are a good source of inexpensive art). Ask the children questions about the characters and setting: *What is the little girl looking at? How do you think she feels? What is the man doing? Where are they?* Urge the children to use their imaginations and think of dialogue for the characters and additional scenes.

Put the students' comments on the blackboard under the heading *My Opinion Is Important.* Make them understand that the activity is an open-ended one, with no right or wrong answers. Progress to more abstract works such as those by Monet, Picasso, Van Gogh.

Song Writing

Whatever the topic you're studying, put the information you want the children to know to music. Choose a well-known tune such as "Jingle Bells." Make it a class effort and have the children help you with the lyrics. The secret is it doesn't have to rhyme!

> Rocks are hard, rocks are soft.
>
> Rocks are smooth and rough.
>
> Some are big and some are small;
>
> They're used in many ways.
>
> We build with them, we polish them
>
> We wear them for jewelry.
>
> Rocks are here, rocks are there.
>
> Rocks are everywhere.

Logical-Mathematical Intelligence

Directed Drawing

Teach the children to look at the elements of shape in the world around them. Have them look for circles, curved lines, straight lines, and angled lines.

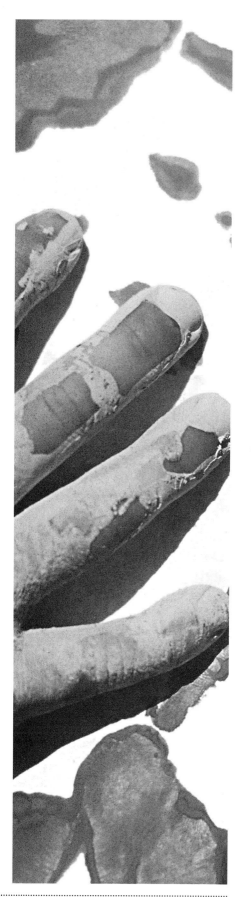

Practice making these shapes on scratch paper. Point out the shapes that make up the window in your classroom, the clock, or the door. Have the children describe what shapes are in their everyday environment.

Choose a picture of an animal that you are studying. Give each child a piece of 9-by-12-inch white construction paper and a fine line black marker. Tape a piece of paper to the chalkboard. Starting with the nose of the animal, draw the animal on your paper while thinking aloud, "This dog's nose is a small shape. Is it a round dot or an oval?" After you draw the nose, instruct the children to draw the nose. Continue with the eyes, face, etc., drawing each feature, then waiting for the children to draw. Encourage the "no talking while we're drawing" rule.

As you draw, look for the shapes in the animal. The beak of an owl is a triangle. The face of an owl and its eyes are circles. Break the picture up into its parts as you draw it, and this will help curb the frustration of children who feel they can't draw. Tell them they can because they can draw dots, circles, lines, etc.

Weaving

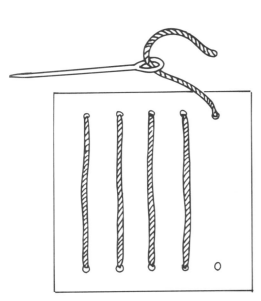

Children will be exposed to the mathematical concepts of measurement, spacing, and patterning as they make their own weaving to hang on a wall.

Each student will need the following materials:

- an eight-inch-square of cardboard or foam
- colored yarn and ribbon
- a pencil
- a plastic darning needle (with a large eye)
- scissors
- a ruler
- masking tape

Demonstrate for students how to use the ruler on the square board to make evenly spaced holes for the foundation strands. Place the ruler at the top of the board and mark off two-inch increments. Poke a hole with the pencil across the top of the board at these points. Do the same on the opposite end of the board. Remind students to make sure the holes line up on the top and bottom of the board.

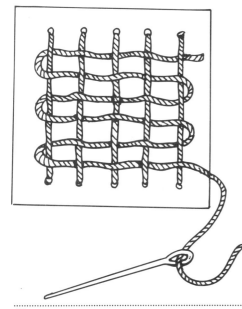

Have students thread a plastic darning needle with yarn or ribbon. Show them how to make a series of straight strands across the board using the pencil holes. Secure the yarn ends with knots or masking tape. Explain that these strands are called the *warp*. Students will weave other strands of yarn—or *weft*—across the board. The weft should be woven over one strand, under the next, and so on. The weft can be woven across the warp, turned around and woven in the other direction. Students should weave the yarn, creating a pattern of colors and textures, until the wall weaving is complete.

Color Addition

For a class painting activity, have students experiment with mixing primary colors—red, yellow, and blue, plus white. Let them mix different colors while you ask question such as:

What will happen if you mix blue and yellow?

What will happen if you put just a little blue in the yellow?

What happens if you mix white with red?

Explain what a number sentence is by giving examples such as 1 + 1 = 2. Have them make addition number sentences with their paint and a pencil. For example: a red dot of paint + a white dot of paint = a pink dot of paint.

Bodily-Kinesthetic Intelligence

Daffy Dough

In this activity, students will make the dough and then work it with their hands to form a piece of art.

To make enough Daffy Dough for the whole class, you will need a large container of Elmer's Glue-All, liquid starch, measuring cups, a large plastic bowl, and a wooden spoon. You may want to add some food coloring to give the dough an interesting color. Have students take turns assisting you as you measure out two cups of Elmer's Glue-All and pour it into the plastic bowl. Then measure out one cup of liquid starch. Next, slowly pour about one-quarter cup of the starch into the plastic bowl with the glue. Have a student volunteer slowly stir the mixture together as you add more liquid starch. Have the student keep mixing as you slowly pour in the starch until the entire cup of liquid starch has been added and the mixture has been blended together. If the mixture is sticky to the touch, add more starch. Add food coloring, if desired, and mix thoroughly. Tell students that now the mixture needs to be covered tightly with cellophane wrapping and refrigerated overnight.

The next day, let students pull and cut off pieces of Daffy Dough to squish, twist, and sculpt into a variety of shapes and forms. Encourage them to make balls by swirling the dough between the palms of their hands, to make snake forms by rubbing the dough back and forth on the surface of a table, or to make a pinch pot by sticking a thumb into a dough ball and then pinching the sides to form the pot. Provide rolling pins, cookie cutters, and plastic knives to inspire them to shape, sculpt, and mold more masterpieces. Follow through with **Daffy Dough Color Words** worksheet on page 66.

page 66

Visual-Spatial Intelligence

Lacy Lantern

To make a lantern, you will need the following materials:

- a clean, one- or two-liter plastic soda bottle for each student
- construction paper in different colors
- glue
- two-inch-wide construction-paper strips
- a nail
- a pencil
- yellow tissue paper
- crayons or colored markers

Have each student bring an empty, clean, one- or two-liter plastic soda bottle from home. Help students remove any paper labels and glue from the bottles. Tell students to choose a piece of construction paper in a color they like. Have students wrap the construction paper around the soda bottle and overlap the ends. Help students to glue the ends in place, taking care not to glue the construction paper to the bottle. While they are waiting for the glue to dry, students can use crayons or colored markers to draw designs on the construction paper.

Once the glue has dried, have students bring you their bottles so you can make holes in the bottles with a nail. Place the bottle down on a small pile of paper towels to hold it in place. Then use a nail to poke a series of holes all around the bottle to create a place for the "light" to shine through the lanterns. After the holes have been made, help each student slide the construction-paper circle off the small end of the bottle. Show students how to use a pencil or crayon to enlarge the holes a little. Then help students to glue the yellow tissue paper to the inside of the construction paper circle to create the "light" of the lantern.

To finish the lanterns, have each student glue a strip of construction paper to the top of the lantern to form a handle. Then have students march in a lantern parade around the classroom.

Color by Code

Have the children color by code to find a mystery picture! Give them a copy of page 67, the **Color by Code** worksheet. Have them color each square according to its symbol. The key is at the top of the page. Review the spelling of the color words with them before they do the activity. *Growing Colors,* by

---

Name_____

Color by Code

Color each square by following the code. Can you discover the mystery picture?

Code: Y = yellow B = blue R = red G = green

B	B	B	B	B	B
B	B	B	Y	B	B
B	B	Y	R	Y	B
B	G	B	Y	B	G
B	B	G	G	G	B
B	B	B	G	B	B

FS23279 Multiple Intelligences Kindergarten   reproducible   67

page 67

Bruce McMillan (Mulberry, 1988), and *Planting a Rainbow,* by Lois Ehlert (Harcourt, Brace, Jovanovich, 1988), are good resources to teach color.

Stamp Prints

Printing with stamps and paint is a fun and exciting art activity for young children. In this activity, students will explore the prints made by a variety of objects.

Divide students into groups of five or six students. Provide each group with the following materials:

- construction paper
- four aluminum pie pans
- tempera paint
- paint smocks
- paper towels
- a wide variety of printing tools—cookie cutters, toy cars, thread spools, a potato masher, egg whip, slotted spoon, berry basket, leaves, broccoli, potato halves, apple halves, grapes, leaves, ferns, twigs, etc.

Have each group work on a table covered with old newspaper. Place two or three folded paper towels in each pie pan. Pour enough paint into the shallow pans to saturate the paper towels. The paper towels will act as a stamp pad to evenly disburse paint onto the printing tool. Provide red, yellow, green, and blue paints for each group of students.

Have each student put on a paint smock. Then give each student a sheet of construction paper. Show students how to use the printing tools—dipping them into the paint and pressing them on the paper. Encourage students to experiment with and make predictions about the printing capabilities of each print tool.

 Musical Intelligence

Walk Like the Animals

Discuss with the children the different ways that animals move. Some animals walk on all four legs. Some animals hop. Some swim using flippers and tails. Some animals fly; others slither. Use a drum or sticks to beat out a rhythm. Tell the children to walk like a bear while you beat the drum. Have them hop like a rabbit while you beat the drum. Have the children move slowly, then quickly; have them wiggle on their tummies like snakes, and fly like birds. Encourage their movements with the drum beat.

Interpersonal Intelligence

Class Totem Pole

Explain to your class that totem poles are carved from tall trees by Indians of the Pacific Northwest. Indian clans were represented by certain animals, birds, fish, or plants. American Indians carved these natural emblems on the totem poles. The tribe held a feast when the totem poles were put up.

The animals represent different values to the Indians. Some of the animals and the values they represent are: bear–strength, goat–fairness and kindness, raven–respecting environmental cleanliness. *Totem Pole,* by Diane Hoyt-Goldsmith (Holiday House, 1990) is a good source of information about totems.

Have children make their own totem poles with milk cartons and oatmeal boxes. They can paint a picture of an animal they like on the carton or box. Attach the boxes to each other with tape or glue and put them on a base made from a large cardboard box.

Class Bouquet

Have your class create a cooperative piece of art to illustrate the concept "two heads are better than one." Explain to them that many creative efforts are done by groups of people who work together. Examples are musical groups, symphonies, quartets, etc.; films created by the many different people in a crew; quilts made by groups of women in quilting bees; and so on.

Create a class bouquet by having children make flowers with different colors of construction paper. Instruct them to make stems for their flowers. Have them make their flowers large enough to write their names on them. Put a large vase on a bulletin board display, and when the children have completed their flowers, have them bring them up to the bulletin board one at a time and glue them into the vase.

Another way to do this activity is to have each child glue a photo of her- or himself on the flower.

Intrapersonal Intelligence

I Show My Feelings

Gather a variety of photographs or drawings that show human emotions. Point out that the lines and curves we see in people's faces give us clues about what they feel. A bright smile tells us that the person is feeling happy. A mouth formed into a straight line probably means that the person is mad. A frown means that the person is unhappy or sad. A wide open mouth with arched eyebrows and big round eyes might mean surprise or fright.

Pair up students. Have one partner make a face to show an emotion such as fear, anger, happiness, sadness, or surprise. The partner should guess the emotion. Let the students switch roles after doing several expressions.

Naturalist Intelligence

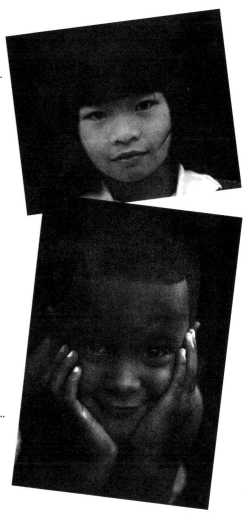

Texture Collage

Give students large sheets of thin paper and crayons. Take the class outside and have them make texture rubbings of different colors. Students lay the sheet of paper over textured surfaces, such as tree bark, weathered wood, leaves, brick, or cement, and rub across the sheet with the side of a crayon. Have the students do several rubbings. Make a large collage mural with the rubbings.

Create a Mini-Meadow

In this activity you will create a small edible "meadow." Obtain alfalfa or clover sprout seeds for growing edible sprouts. You will also need cotton to sprout the seeds in. Create a natural-looking setting for your sprout meadow with clay. With your class, make trees, flowers, shrubs, a fence, a scarecrow, etc. Real rocks and twigs can also be used.

Spread the cotton across a large, flat baking tin. Dampen the cotton by spraying it with water. Sprinkle the seeds onto the cotton. Surround the area with your setting.

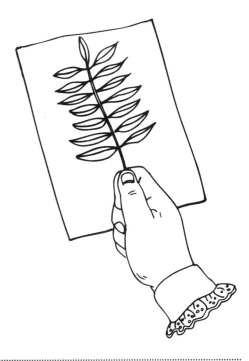

Place the mini-meadow in a sunny window. Make sure the seeds do not dry out. When they have formed small leaves and obtained a length of 1 to 2 inches, "harvest" the sprouts. Add them to a tossed salad or egg salad served on crackers and enjoy with your class.

Name_____

Daffy Dough Color Words

Roll your dough into a long thin
shape and place it on top of
the letters of the color words.

red

blue

yellow

green

reproducible

FINE ARTS   Bodily-Kinesthetic Intelligence

Color by Code

Color each square by following the code. Can you discover the mystery picture?

Code: Y = yellow   B = blue   R = red   G = green

B	B	B	B	B	B	B
B	B	B	Y	B	B	B
B	B	Y	R	Y	B	B
B	G	B	Y	B	G	B
B	B	G	G	G	B	B
B	B	B	G	B	B	B
B	B	B	B	B	B	B

reproducible

FINE ARTS
Visual-Spatial Intelligence

Verbal-Linguistic Intelligence

Shoot to Spell

Have several players gather around a basketball hoop with one basketball, a mini-chalkboard, and a piece of chalk. Their job is to work together to spell a word. It can be a spelling word or a vocabulary word from a unit they are studying. Provide the children with a list of words to use. To spell the word, the children must "earn" the letters. To earn a letter, the players must make a basket. The players take turns shooting the ball. When one of them makes a basket, he or she writes the first letter of the word on the chalkboard. Play continues until all the letters have been earned and the word is spelled. All the players win! Then have the children choose a new word, and play resumes.

The Athlete Says...

In this activity, students will explore the athletic moves needed for a number of different sports as they engage their listening skills. First discuss different sports and the movements made in them, such as: a football player making a pass, a tennis player serving a ball, a basketball player bouncing a ball, etc. Have students practice making each movement.

In an open area of the playground, form a large circle to play a sports version of "Simon Says." Each student will get to say a sports move, such as, "The athlete says to kick the soccer ball." Tell the students who are watching to listen for the student volunteer to say the words "The athlete says" before they make the same move. Explain to them that if the student doesn't say those words, they should not make the move. Let students take turns in the role of "Athlete Says."

Logical-Mathematical Intelligence

Jump Like a Frog

In this activity, students will attempt to see who can jump the farthest. Teach the class about measurement with the **Jump Like a Frog** worksheet on page 76. Then take students outside to a grassy area. Tell students that they are going to pretend to be frogs. Explain that they will plant both feet on the ground, bend down, and lean forward so that their hands are on the ground. When they are in this position, they will kick off with their legs and try to leap as far forward as they can. Encourage students to practice their jumps a few times, until they feel like confident frog jumpers.

Make a large chart on cardboard and write each student's name on it. (Student's will log their best jumps on the chart.) Provide a measuring tape or yard stick so that students can measure the distance of their jumps. Place the measuring tape or yard stick on the ground and weigh it down so that it does not move. Lay out a marker of yarn on the ground at the beginning of the measuring tape to mark the starting point for the jumps. Then have students take turns making their frog jumps and measuring the length of their jumps. Point out the inch numbers on the measuring tape and help students count the number of inches jumped. Have students record the length of their best frog jump on the class chart.

Ask students the following question: Does the length of your legs have anything to do with the length of your frog jump? Encourage students to think about this question and discuss their thoughts.

Who Is Gone?

Have the children set up their chairs in a big circle and sit down. Put one chair in the middle of the circle. Choose a child to be "It." Have "It" sit in the chair in the middle of the circle, blindfold him or her, and have him or her cover his or her ears. After this is done, tap another child on the shoulder. That child should disappear behind a bookcase or any hidden spot. While he or she is hiding, have the rest of the children switch places quickly and silently. Then take the blindfold off "It" and ask him or her to name the person who is missing. Give "It" three guesses. If "It" guesses correctly, the hidden child returns to the big circle and "It" gets to choose who will be "It" next. If, after three guesses, "It" doesn't know, have the hidden child come out. That child gets to be "It" and the guessing child returns to the big circle.

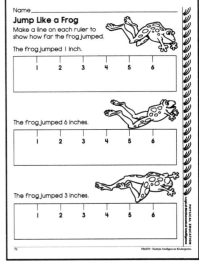

page 76

Bodily-Kinesthetic Intelligence

Don't Break the Snake

Children have to walk in a line often at school. Whether it is going into the classroom, going out for a fire drill, or lining up to go to an assembly, the concept of "single file" must be taught.

A fun way to practice walking in a single file line is to play "Don't Break the Snake." Take the children outdoors. Have them line up in a single file so they

are looking at the back of the head of the person in front of them. Announce to them that they are now a snake. Go to the front of the line to be the head of the snake. The last people in line are the tail of the snake. The object of the game is to not break the snake. Begin walking with the children following you. Walk in a circle and in an S-formation. Go faster and faster until you are leading the children on a crazy, zigzag path, all the while calling out, "Don't break the snake!" The children must be aware of the children in front of them and behind them.

Remind the children that snakes don't talk, and they don't have hands so they can't touch each other. Playing several sessions of this game will help children walk in a single-file line better. A simple reminder of "Don't break the snake" helps them focus on each other and their line when walking somewhere as a class.

Following the Course

Obstacle courses offer children an opportunity to challenge their physical abilities and their understanding of directions. In this activity, students will enjoy performing active movements and learning about the spatial relationships on the obstacle course.

You'll need a stack of carpet squares, chalk, a balance beam, two or three bean bags, and a bucket. Set out a trail of three or four carpet squares on a flat surface on the playground. At the end of the trail, draw a hopscotch diagram. Students will count each hop out loud as they hop through the hopscotch diagram.

Start another short trail of carpet squares from the hopscotch diagram that leads to a wide wooden balance beam laid directly on the ground. Students will walk across the balance beam, heel to toe to the end of the beam. Place several more carpet squares on the ground at the end of the balance beam to guide students to the next obstacle on the course. Set two or three bean bags next to the last carpet square, and place a bucket about three feet from the square. Have students stand on the last square and try to pitch the bean bags into the bucket. Tell students they must get all three bean bags into the bucket in order to complete the course. As students complete the obstacle course, give them a sticker or a reward badge.

Visual-Spatial Intelligence

Just Like Me

Children play this game in pairs. Have two children face each other. One person is "Me;" the other is "Just Like Me." The person who is Me makes a face. Then the other child mimics this. The person who is Me raises his or her hand and wiggles the fingers. The other child does the same. Tell the children they are imagining they are looking into a mirror. The mirror reflects the action as the person looking into the mirror does it. Have the children take turns being "Me" and "Just Like Me."

Musical Intelligence

Do the Yankee Doodle!

Sing the lyrics below to the tune of "Yankee Doodle," keeping the rhythm with a drum or sticks, and have the children perform what you sing:

All the children stood right up,

then they started jumping,

jumped up high, then jumped so low,

then they started skipping.

All the children skipped around

in a great big circle,

skipped quite fast and then slowed down,

then they started clapping.

All the children clapped their hands,

loudly, then so softly,

clapped until they sat right down,

and folded their hands neatly.

Rhythm and Rhyme

When children jump rope and skip, rhythm helps them to do the activity successfully. In this activity, students will add rhythm to their jumping and skipping by chanting rhymes as they move.

Teach students this familiar rhyme to use as they learn to jump rope, to skip, to throw and catch a ball, or do some other rhythmic movement. Have students chant the rhyme together as they move to the beat.

Teddy Bear

Teddy Bear, Teddy Bear, turn around.

Teddy Bear, Teddy Bear, touch the ground.

Teddy Bear, Teddy Bear, show your nose.

Teddy Bear, Teddy Bear, that will do!

Teddy Bear, Teddy Bear, go upstairs.

Teddy Bear, Teddy Bear, say your prayers.

Teddy Bear, Teddy Bear, turn out the lights.

Teddy Bear, Teddy Bear, say good night!

Interpersonal Intelligence

Line Soccer

Divide the class into two teams. Draw two chalk lines on the blacktop about 25 feet away from each other. Have each team line up on a chalk line facing the other team. Put a soccer ball in the middle of the two teams. Make an X to mark the ball's spot. Give each child on each team a number or a letter (you can write them on slips of paper). Use the same numbers or letters for both teams. Call out a number or a letter. (It helps to keep track of the ones you've called by jotting them down.) The children who have that number or letter run to the ball and, without using their hands, try to kick the ball through the opposing team's line. The children waiting on the line try to kick the ball back into the field of play. If a child kicks the ball through the line, his team scores a point. The ball must stay on the ground—no "fly" balls.

Tablecloth Activities

In these activities, students will work with a tablecloth. You'll need a few large round tablecloths, masking tape, and a small bouncing ball for each student. Cut a strip of masking tape long enough for each student to print his or her name on it. Have students attach their name tapes to their bouncy balls.

First do some warm-up activities. Put the tablecloths flat on the ground and have the students stand around them, about five to a tablecloth. Have the students lift the tablecloth over their heads and back down again. Then have the students practice holding the tablecloth with one hand and walking around in a circle. Have them switch hands and walk the other way, and then run in a circle. They can also skip and walk backward.

Bouncing Balls: Spread the tablecloths out on the floor and have each group of students stand around one tablecloth. Tell each group to grab hold of the tablecloth and lift it up to their waists. Have them place their bouncing balls on the tablecloth, making sure the balls don't immediately roll off the edge. Then tell them to lift the tablecloth over their heads, holding on to the edges with both hands. Have them move the tablecloth up and down, trying to keep the balls on the tablecloth and away from the edges, where they will fall to the ground. Tell the groups that the winner is the person whose bouncy ball is the last left on the tablecloth.

Run for It: Students hold the parachute at waist level. Have one student at a time let go of the tablecloth when a leader blows a whistle, and run under it. This student should take the tablecloth from a student. That student should then run under the tablecloth when the whistle blows again, and take the tablecloth from another person, and so on.

Under a Cloud: Tell the students to lift the tablecloth over their heads. When the leader blows the whistle, students should sit down and let the tablecloth fall on them.

Charades

On slips of paper, write different physical activities, such as:

Wash the dishes

Sweep the floor

Hoe the garden

Dig a hole

Row a boat

Swim in a pool

Surf on a surfboard

Run a race

Skate on ice

Climb a tree

Drive a car

Play basketball

Eat a giant sandwich

Act like a monkey (elephant, seal, snake, penguin, etc.)

Invite a child to come up in front of the class and choose a slip of paper. Whisper the activity into the child's ear so the rest of the class won't hear. Then have the child act it out, while the rest of the class copies him. The children should guess what they are doing. The child who guesses first gets to choose and act out the next charade.

Intrapersonal Intelligence

Dance and Float

Young children enjoy moving to the rhythm of music, especially when they can use props that help them see the flow of music. In this activity, students will use lightweight fabric scarves to enhance their creative movements.

Each student will need a lightweight square of fabric or a scarf that will float gently when moved. Encourage students to toss the scarves into the air and watch them slowly and lightly float to the ground. Have students experiment with the amount of force necessary to send the scarves high into the air and the easy movement of the fabric trailing behind them as they skip, jump, or run.

After students have had an opportunity to experiment with the scarves, move to an open area suitable for large movements. Alternate playing recordings of soft and slow, fast and active, and loud and powerful music for students to move to as they express themselves with the scarves.

Classical music selections that will work well include:

- Bach's *Sleepers Awake*
- Chopin's *Minute Waltz*
- Mozart's *Eine kleine Nachtmusik*
- Pachelbel's *Canon*
- Rimsky-Korsakoff's *Scheherazade*
- Sousa marches
- Tchaikovsky's *Waltz of the Flowers*

Encourage students to move their bodies and scarves in time to the flow or beat of the music. Have students discuss their movements and their feelings after the exercise.

Tune in to Yourself

After physical activity, or in the middle of a rainy day, invite the children to lie on the carpet and close their eyes. Put on some quiet, soothing music. In a gentle voice, tell them to tune in to themselves. Have them breathe deeply into their abdomens, letting the air out slowly. To help them relax, suggest any of the following:

- You are on a sailboat on a lake. The wind is pushing you along gently. The wind is dying down, and you are moving slower, and slower, and slower . . .

- You are a snowman on a hot day, melting . . . melting . . . melting. . . .

- You are drifting off in a hot-air balloon, over a sunny meadow.
- You have no backbone. You are floating in a warm pool that is gently rocking you.

Then say the following to the students in a calm, slow voice.

Relax.

Rest your toes. Rest your feet.

Rest your knees. Rest your legs.

Rest your hips. Rest your back.

Rest your tummy. Rest your shoulders.

Rest your fingers. Rest your arms.

Rest your neck. Rest your head.

Rest your eyes. Rest your mouth.

Rest your tongue. Rest your forehead.

Breathe in deeply. Let the air out slowly.

Let the children relax for a few minutes, simply enjoying the music. When it's time to get up, reverse the process, saying, "Wake your toes. Wake your feet ..."

Naturalist Intelligence

Animal Movements

This activity engages children's knowledge of animal movements as well as their listening skills. Think of several animal movements that students can do and remember easily. Have the class practice them, following your example. Some movements could be:

- A duck flying. Flap arms up and down at sides.
- A rabbit hopping. With hands held at chest level, take short hops.
- A penguin waddling. Keep ankles close together and shuffle.

When you say "ducks fly" to the class, they should all fly on cue until you tell them to stop. Next say something like "dogs fly." The class should remain motionless. Continue with all the animal movements. Have children take turns playing the role of leader.

Jump Like a Frog

Make a line on each ruler to
show how far the frog jumped.

The frog jumped 1 inch.

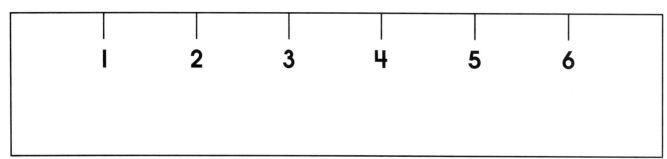

The frog jumped 6 inches.

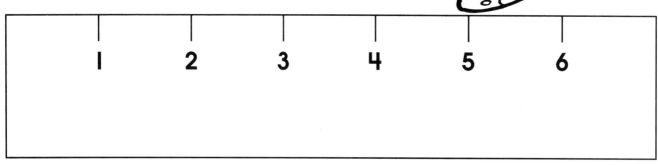

The frog jumped 3 inches.

reproducible   FS23279 · Multiple Intelligences Kindergarten